THE SOVIET UNION

World Education Series

The Soviet Union

J. J. TOMIAK
*Hayter Lecturer in Russian and Soviet Education,
Institute of Education and School of Slavonic and
East European Studies, University of London*

ARCHON BOOKS   Hamden   Connecticut

Library of Congress Cataloging in Publication Data

Tomiak, J   J
      The Soviet Union
      (World education series)
      Bibliography: p.
      1. Education—Russia—History.   I. Title.
LA832.T6   370'.947   72-1529
ISBN 0-208-01302-4

Contents

5

CHAPTER 2: ADMINISTRATION, FINANCE
AND PLANNING

Foreword

THE aim of this book is to inform those who are interested in education or in Soviet affairs of the growth, development and the present state of education in the USSR.

A modest book of this size cannot aim at a thorough analysis of the Soviet educational system or a rigorous examination of the background influences which have been shaping it over the course of the last fifty years. My task has rather been to provide the essential up-to-date information for all those who feel that education, far from being a matter of individual concern, is of crucial importance to society and its cultural and economic growth, as well as for those who are now convinced that whatever happens in the largest country of the world, under a political system which has spread to cover a third of the whole globe, cannot be ignored.

I have tried to describe and explain the working of an important part of the social system of a country in a way in which a technician describes and explains the working of a complicated mechanism. But one cannot forget that the mechanism under consideration here is a vital part of a living organism, in fact it is both its brain and its heart. The knowledge of how Soviet education works is the key to a better understanding of the life of the Soviet society as a whole in the past, at present and in the future; in other words, to the understanding of one of the crucial elements in our modern world.

J.J.T.

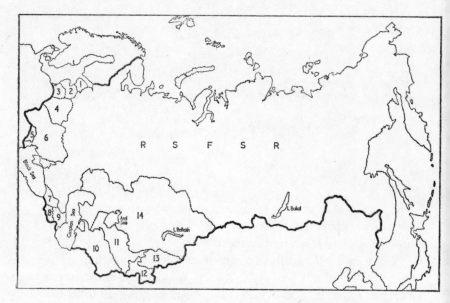

1 Estonia	8 Armenia
2 Latvia	9 Azerbaidzhan
3 Lithuania	10 Turkmenistan
4 Byelorussia	11 Uzbekistan
5 Moldavia	12 Tadzhikstan
6 Ukraine	13 Kirghizstan
7 Georgia	14 Kazakhstan

Note

An attempt to establish any equivalents of the rouble in terms of foreign currencies must be approached with extreme caution, owing to the wide differences in the structures of prices and wages obtaining in the different types of economic set-up and the arbitrary character of the official rates of exchange between the rouble and other currencies, which do not reflect the true nature of the relationship.

Only as a very rough guide one may take the official rates of exchange which at the beginning of October 1971 were:

£ = 2.20 roubles
US $ = 0.90 roubles
Canadian $ = 0.8878 roubles
Australian $ = 1.01 roubles
New Zealand $ = 1.01 roubles
(*Izvestia*, No 235 (16853), 5 October 1971)

I

The Roots of the Soviet Educational System

HISTORICAL BACKGROUND

ON 25 October 1917 the Bolshevik revolutionaries seized the Winter Palace in St Petersburg. Kerensky's Provisional Government was overthrown. The Military Revolutionary Committee issued a proclamation stating that the power had passed into the hands of the Soviet of Workers' and Soldiers' Deputies. The following day the Government of People's Commissars was established. Communist power was no longer a dream. It had become a reality.

The Bolsheviks inherited a country which was retarded in its social, political and economic development. Educationally it was characterised by a high degree of illiteracy, socially conditioned educational opportunities at all levels of education, an ill-conceived administrative dualism between the secular and the ecclesiastical authorities and the inability of the government to enforce free and universal elementary education. In addition, the Tsarist authorities persistently used the schools to foster the Russianisation of the national minorities within the country.

Education under war communism (1918–21) The new Soviet government quickly began to introduce a series of fundamental educational reforms. In December 1917 the Council of People's Commissars promulgated a decree which transferred all the primary, secondary and higher schools in the country to the People's Commissariat of Education (*Narkompros*) which replaced the former Ministry of Education. The first Commissar of Education was the literary critic Anatoly V. Lunacharsky. *Narkompros* was organised into seventeen departments, dealing with universal compulsory education, universities and establishments of higher education, home education and people's universities, aid to independent school organisations, experimental pedagogy, school medicine and hygiene, technical schools and polytechnic education, construction of new schools and literature and publishing.

The decree of the Council of People's Commissars of 23 January 1918 separated the church from the state and the school from the church. The teaching of religious doctrines in schools was prohibited. The school became a secular institution. At the same time the national minorities obtained the right to instruction in the native languages. Women were given equal rights, including equal right to education at all levels.

The decree of the All-Russian Central Executive Committee of the Council of Deputies of 16 October 1918 declared the Basic Principles of Uniform Schooling for Workers. All schools were to belong to the people. They were to be fully accessible to all children of both sexes, and instruction was to be free. The whole system of schools from kindergarten to university was declared to constitute one school, one unbroken ladder. The basic link was to be a universal, free, compulsory, secular and undifferentiated school with a general nine-year course of instruction, consisting of a first level of five years and a second level of four years. The plan was as ambitious as it was radical.

Another important measure was the Decree on the Entrance Rules to Higher School, signed by Lenin on 2 August 1918. Under these any person who had reached the age of sixteen, of whatever citizenship or nationality and of either sex, was entitled to be admitted into any institution of higher learning without submitting any certificate of graduation from a secondary or any other school. The only requirements were identity cards and birth certificates. All tuition fees were abolished.

The Eighth Congress of the Russian Communist Party in March 1919 laid down the fundamental aims and principles of the Soviet educational system. This was to consist of pre-school institutions such as nurseries, kindergartens and children's homes, free and compulsory schools for all children of both sexes between eight and seventeen years of age, and universities and other institutions of higher education which were to be open to all who desired to study at this level. The teachers were to be imbued with ideas of communism, and education out of school was to expand to embrace libraries, schools for adults, people's palaces and universities, cinemas and theatres. The state was to supply all pupils with food, clothes, boots and free school aids. The programme greatly exceeded the real possibilities of a poor country, devastated by war.

The opening of universities to all without any special qualifications made it necessary to create special facilities for preparatory studies of some kind. By the decree of the People's Commissariat of Education of 11 September 1919, the Workers' Faculties (*Rabfaks*) came into being in the form of preparatory courses organised at the higher schools. They radically altered the social composition of the student body in the universities in the following years. In 1925, 38·5 per cent of all students enrolled in the universities had come from the Workers' Faculties.

On 26 December 1919 Lenin, as President of the Council of People's Commissars, signed the Decree on the Elimination of Illiteracy among the Population of the RSFSR. The decree made it compulsory for the entire population of the republic between the ages of eight and fifty to learn to read and write in Russian or in the native language. It provided for a two-hour reduction in the working day, without loss in wages, for those attending schools for reading and writing. An intensive publicity campaign was undertaken to persuade the illiterate that it was their basic civic duty to master the two fundamental skills, and to impress upon the literate that it was their duty to actively help in the speedy achievement of universal literacy. As a result, Party, Komsomol and trade union workers, teachers and others joined in the literacy campaign. An All-Russian Extraordinary Commission for the Elimination of Illiteracy was established. In 1920 over 12,000 literacy centres (*likpunkty*) were operating in the European part of the RSFSR. According to the figures published by the Extraordinary Commission, by July 1921 4·8 million people had been taught to read and write, most of them Red

Army soldiers. In 1923 a voluntary society, Down with Illiteracy (*Doloy negramotnost*), was formed to support the work of the movement for the liquidation of illiteracy (*likbez*) in both the Russian and non-Russian areas. It was not, however, till the late 1930s that the point of almost complete literacy among the adult population was reached. In 1939, 95 per cent of men and 83 per cent of women were literate.

Education and the New Economic Policy (1921–7)   On 11 February 1921 the Council of People's Commissars of the RSFSR issued a decree on the Establishment of Institutes of Red Professors in Moscow and Petrograd. These were organised to train professors and lecturers in political economy, historical materialism, modern history and Soviet government. Prominent as teachers in the Institutes were old communist intellectuals: Anatoly Lunacharsky, Mikhail Pokrovsky, Vyacheslav Volgin, Nikolai Semashko, Vladimir Bonch Bruyevich and Panteleimon Lepeshinsky. The first Red Professors graduated from the Institutes in the summer of 1924.

On 2 September 1921 the Council of People's Commissars endorsed the Statute of the Institutions of Higher Learning in the RSFSR which declared the aims and tasks of the Soviet higher education establishments. It specified, among other things, that the instructors and scientific workers could be elected by the higher school councils by a show of hands and recommended to the State Learned Council for professorial appointments without a degree or a title. This extreme measure was designed to speed up the process of bringing the younger radical intellectuals to positions of power and influence in higher education, and put the political before any other considerations.

In August 1923 the Council of People's Commissars prepared a plan for introducing universal primary education on a compulsory basis for the whole country. It was to be completed within the following decade. By that time it was becoming clear that the strength of an ideology alone could never accomplish grandiose egalitarian plans for which an abundance of capital, highly qualified personnel and other resources were absolutely indispensable. The process of coming to terms with the gruesome

reality was a painful one. The dreams of a spectacular progress
began to turn into the nightmare of regression. In the first months
of 1921 the number of primary schools was estimated at between
76,000 and 82,000 with 6 to 6·8 million pupils. By April 1922 the
number of schools had dropped to 68,000; by December 1922, to
55,000; by October 1923, to 49,000 with 3·7 million pupils.[1] This
looked like a calamity. Exhausted by the war, the Revolution, and
foreign intervention, as well as incapacitated by the lack of capital,
the stoppage of industrial production and a steep decline in
agricultural output, the country was facing disaster. In education,
the most cherished plans had to be abandoned. Early in 1923 the
Council of the People's Commissars sanctioned the introduction
of fees at all levels of education with the exemption of certain
categories of pupils. One of the fundamental principles of communist education—the right to free education—ceased to apply.

In 1926 there was, however, some improvement and industrial
production was, roughly, back to the pre-war (1913) level. This
continued in 1927 and 1928. The New Economic Policy was
bearing fruit, while Stalin's doctrine of 'socialism in one country'
and a ruthless programme of industrialisation provided the necessary 'Soviet atheistic equivalent of the Protestant Ethic'.[2]

The middle 1920s produced many interesting innovations and
ideas in educational thought. Pavel Blonsky's *Labour School*
(*Trudovaya Shkola*), which had appeared in 1919 but gained
popularity only a few years later, insisted that productive work
and socially useful labour were the basis of all education. The
significance of labour and work in a collective were stressed by
Stanislav Shatsky. Viktor Shulgin's radical theories went even
further: he envisaged the ultimate 'withering away of the school',
with the artificial lines of division between school and life completely removed. Lenin kept Blonsky's book in his library;
Lenin's wife, Nadezhda Krupskaya, popularised Marx's ideas on
the combination of productive labour and instruction and on
polytechnic education, the latter being the theoretical and practical familiarisation with the general principles of industrial production and the main branches of industry. A new psychological
orientation produced pedology, a new science derived from the

elements of psychology and pedagogy or, in the words of Albert
Pinkevich, the author of *Experience of Marxist Pedagogy* (*Opyt
Marksistskoy Pedagogiki*), 'a science . . . concerned with the
psychological and physical development of the child from birth
to maturity'.[3] The First All-Union Congress of Pedology in
December 1927 was attended by 2,500 participants. Krupskaya,
Lunacharsky and the philosopher Nikolai Bukharin were the
principal speakers.

Education under the first three Five-Year Plans (1928–42)
The first three Five-Year Plans transformed the USSR from an
agricultural country with almost totally unutilised resources into
a mixed economy, bent upon rapid industrialisation. The First
Five-Year Plan (1928–32) aimed rigorously at increasing capital
investment in the heavy industry at the expense of consumption,
but also paid attention to developing education as one of the
factors conditioning industrial growth.

At the Sixteenth Congress of the Communist Party, early in
1930, a decision was taken to press on with the introduction of
compulsory universal primary education in the country. A decision of the Central Executive Committee and the USSR Council of Ministers in August 1930 declared that education was
compulsory for all boys and girls from the age of eight for at
least a four-year course of primary schooling. A decision was also
taken at the same time to introduce universal compulsory schooling for boys and girls up to the age of fourteen in industrial
towns, as from the school year 1930/1.

A decree of 8 April 1929 codified all the previous regulations
concerning the religious influences upon the young into a general
law on the subject. The teaching of any kind of religious belief
was once more strictly forbidden in all types of school. The
Society of Militant Atheists, which had been formed in 1925,
intensified its anti-religious activities with the help of the
periodical *Atheist in the School* (*Bezbozhnik v Shkole*).

At its plenary meeting in November 1929 the Central Committee of the Communist Party emphasised the need for more
and better scientists and teachers and, in particular, for training
practical workers with an adequate theoretical background. The

institutions of higher learning and the research establishments were directed to change their methods of selection and put much greater stress upon academic contests and scientific competition. It became clear that the attempt to increase industrial and agricultural output had to begin with an all-out effort to produce the necessary technologists, scientists and engineers. To facilitate this process *Narkompros* adopted in 1930 special regulations under which several supervisory functions in connection with postgraduate training were transferred from the central authority of the Commissariat directly to the institutions of higher learning and research. The rectors and directors of the higher education establishments and research institutes became personally responsible for the selection and training of scientific manpower. Yet the future scientists also had to be political activists: in 1931, 48·4 per cent of the postgraduate students were members of the Party or the Komsomol. In the academic year 1929/30 the country's higher education institutions and research establishments had more than 3,000 postgraduate students, nearly two and a half times the number in 1927/8. The foundations for an intensive programme of industrial and technological improvement were laid.

On 5 September 1931 the Central Committee of the Party passed a Resolution on the Primary and Secondary School, criticising the inadequate preparation of pupils for studying in the higher education institutions and technical schools. It called for greater efficiency in instructing the young in the schools and was a clear indication of a major policy change.

A year later, a decree of 25 August 1932 on School Programmes and Administration in Primary and Secondary Schools was issued by the Central Committee of the Party. It called in no uncertain words for the strengthening of school discipline and the thorough revision of all courses of study in primary and secondary schools. By that year almost all children aged eight to eleven were receiving full-time education.

In pursuit of the above objectives further decrees were issued. A regulation on Textbooks for the Elementary Schools of 12 February 1933 reinstated the school textbook as a principal teaching

B

aid in the place of the project method and other progressive experiments. In the middle of the next year instructions were issued on the teaching of history and geography in a systematic way, with the view of promoting the materialist world outlook among pupils.

Educational reforms continued in the same spirit and with the same intensity in the period of the Second Five-Year Plan (1933–7). A decree on the Organisation of Educational Work and Inner Order in the Primary, Incomplete Secondary and Secondary Schools introduced and defined in 1935 a uniform system of grading pupils' progress on a scale from five to one. Grade five (excellent) exempted a candidate for higher education from sitting an entrance examination.

A year earlier a unified system of certification of the scientific and teaching personnel had been introduced for all institutions of higher learning by a decree on Academic Degrees and Titles. Two degrees, those of the Candidate of Science (*Kandidat Nauk*) and the Doctor of Science (*Doktor Nauk*) were universally adopted.

By that time all progressive ideas and methods were looked upon by the political authority with disfavour; indeed they became quite unacceptable. On 4 July 1936 the Central Committee issued its decree on the Pedological Perversions in the System of *Narkompros*. It was the final condemnation of pedology as anti-Marxist and unscientific. Psychological tests were stopped, intelligence tests were also abandoned. Andrei S. Bubnov, the follower of Lunacharsky, was dismissed and Vladimir Potemkin was appointed as the new Commissar of People's Education.

The former educational writers and thinkers disappeared from the scene. Some perished, forgotten in Stalin's labour camps. Their place was taken by Anton S. Makarenko, the famous author of *Road Into Life* (Russian title, *Pedagogicheskaya Poema*), *Flags on the Towers* (*Flagi na Bashnyakh*) and *Books for Parents* (*Knigi dlya Roditeley*). He advocated para-military discipline as a means for strengthening Soviet patriotism and developed the idea of education in and through a collective, after gaining wider reputation as a successful leader of the colonies for young delinquents in the Ukraine in the 1920s.

The Third Five-Year Plan (1938–42), adopted at the Eighteenth Party Congress in March 1939, outlined a plan for the introduction of universal ten-year education in towns and seven-year education in the rural districts. A detailed system was introduced for the registration of children subject to compulsory education and for a strict check on regular attendance. However, in 1940 tuition fees were imposed in higher education and in grades eight to ten in secondary schools.

As the danger of a German invasion increased, a powerful drive was made to prepare large numbers of skilled workers. The order of the Presidium of the Supreme Soviet of 2 October 1940 on the State Labour Reserves of the USSR set up the Chief Administration of Labour Reserves under the Council of the People's Commissars of the USSR. It organised vocational schools with a two-year course of instruction, railway schools to train railway transport workers and six-month training courses in factories (FZO) to prepare skilled workers for the basic industries, such as coalmining, building, iron and steel. Altogether training in over 400 specialised occupations was introduced.

Education during and after World War II (1941–50)　　As a result of the invasion of the USSR by Germany in June 1941, a huge part of the country fell into the hands of the enemy, who reached the foothills of the Caucasus, broke through to the Volga, laid siege to Leningrad and threatened Moscow. The Soviet losses were colossal. Over 20 million people were killed fighting the enemy or perished as civilian population. Over 70,000 towns and villages were reduced to ashes and the country lost nearly 30 per cent of its national wealth.

The war naturally affected educational progress in a direct way. In the territories occupied by the enemy normal work stopped, and in other areas extraordinary measures had to be taken.

In October 1942 the Council of People's Commissars passed two laws on military and physical training of the pupils, in order to familiarise adolescents with the techniques of modern warfare and prepare them for taking part in the struggle against the enemy. In the field of industrial training special vocational schools were organised for children aged twelve and thirteen, many of them war orphans, to give them a four-year course of general education and vocational training combined. Over 2 million young workers were trained in the vocational schools and FZO courses during the war years.

In the middle of the war, on 1 October 1943, a resolution of the Council of the People's Commissars introduced the compulsory education of children from the age of seven, instead of eight, a long overdue reform. In the same year the Academy of Pedagogical Sciences of the RSFSR came into being and a new type of evening school for general education was opened for the working youths who had to interrupt their studies because of the war.

It took the Soviet Union at least five years to restore the material losses caused by the war. Together with the process of reconstruction went further educational reforms. The Chief Administration of Labour Reserves was merged with the Committee for the Registration and Allocation of Manpower to form the All-Union Ministry of Labour Reserves. The network of vocational-technical schools was considerably expanded.

The attention of the Soviet government turned next to the problem of political education. In August 1946 the Central Committee of the Party adopted a decree on the Training and Retraining of Leading Party and Soviet Workers, that is, on the system of Party Schools. The existing schools were reorganised on three levels: the lower Party schools, offering a two-year course and preparing for the lesser positions in the Party; the Higher Party School, founded in 1939, training for the more important positions and, finally, the Academy of Social Sciences, directly under the Central Committee of the Communist Party, an institution of university rank, preparing lecturers in subjects like history, marxism-leninism, political economy, history of philosophy and international relations. Despite the efforts to train enough specialists in these fields, according to the statistics of the Ministry of Higher Education for 1949/50, 238 of the 614 heads of departments of marxism-leninism and 2,201 of the 2,756 lecturers in the subject in higher education establishments had no degree or title.[4] One-year refresher courses were, therefore, organised in 1949 at the universities of Moscow, Leningrad and Kiev for the lecturers in this subject. Their task was to raise the lecturers' qualifications and prepare them for the degree of Candidate of Social Science.

In March 1946 the Supreme Soviet of the USSR approved the Directives on the Fourth Five-Year Plan for reconstructing and developing the national economy in the period 1946–50. The plans proposed to restore and expand the network of primary and secondary schools, to provide universal compulsory education for all children from seven years of age, and to improve the quality of teaching and education in the schools. By 1950 there were in the USSR 200,000 schools of general education with 33·3 million pupils, of whom 7·5 million attended 126,000 small primary schools. The number of seven-year schools rose from 45,700 in the school year 1940/1 to 59,600 in 1950/1. The number of ten-year schools was, however, lagging behind: there were only 15,000 of them with 10·2 million pupils in 1950/1, while there had been 18,800 with 12·2 million pupils in 1940/1. The other branches of the system made a quicker recovery: the secondary specialised education establishments reached the pre-war (1940) level in 1947 and the institutions of higher education accomplished the same in 1948. Co-education was discontinued in the complete secondary schools in the late 1940s and separate schools for boys and girls were introduced in all large towns.

Education during the Fifth and Sixth Five-Year Plans (1951–60) The Fifth Five-Year Plan (1951–5) again put great stress upon the development of heavy industry and increase in agricultural production. In the field of education it provided for an increase in the number of students training to become teachers, improvement and expansion in the teaching of science, a 30–35 per cent increase in the number of students graduating from higher and secondary specialised education establishments and a doubling of the number of graduates in higher education entering the most important branches of industry. While these targets were all achieved in due course, the hope for the introduction of compulsory ten-year education in the towns by 1955 was dashed.

Meanwhile, the Nineteenth Congress of the CPSU in 1952

announced an important decision to reintroduce polytechnic training in schools. In implementing this decision the Ministries of Education of the Union republics and the RSFSR Academy of Pedagogical Sciences began to elaborate the aims and content of polytechnic education, with the help of teachers, scientists and production experts. Traditionally, there were three possible approaches: (1) Lenin's concept of polytechnic education as instruction on electrification of the country coupled with the study of the scientific principles of modern industrial production, its main branches and the fundamentals of industry in general; (2) Krupskaya's idea that polytechnism was not a separate teaching subject, but essentially an approach that should permeate every discipline and be linked with practical activities and especially labour training and, finally (3) the study of the fundamentals of technology and production linked with systematic industrial practice in the factories and on the state and collective farms. The final outcome of the debates was the Khrushchev Memorandum of 1958.

At the beginning of the school year 1956/7 all tuition fees in the upper grades of secondary schools were abolished by order of the Council of Ministers of the USSR, making the whole sequence of primary, secondary and higher education in the country free.

The Twentieth Congress of the CPSU in February 1956 adopted the Directives for the Sixth Five-Year Plan (1956–60). They provided for a substantial increase in the numbers of students who studied in secondary specialised and higher education institutions in the evening or by correspondence without giving up full-time employment. The decision was announced to open new educational establishments for training specialists in many branches of industry in Siberia, Kazakhstan and the Soviet Far East. Another important step was the announcement by Khrushchev in his report to the Congress of the introduction of boarding schools on a large scale. The latter idea was vigorously pursued in the years immediately following the Twentieth Congress, but then, in view of the high costs involved, began to receive less and less attention. Priority had to be given to other, more pressing needs.

In April 1958 Khrushchev addressed the Thirteenth Congress of the Komsomol and announced that it was the duty of the school to prepare each boy and girl for work and to create values useful to men and society, thereby indicating the character of the next reform to come.

On 21 September 1958 an elaborate memorandum by Khrushchev appeared in *Pravda*, in which he criticised the schools for being divorced from life and argued the need for their thorough reform. The following month, on 16 November, the Central Committee of the CPSU and the USSR Council of Ministers issued their Theses on Strengthening the Ties of the School with Life and Further Developing the System of Public Education. The forty-eight theses were a statement on the aims and tasks of Soviet education in the era of rapid scientific and technological progress. They declared the communist transformation of society to be inseparably bound up with 'the education of the new man, in whom spiritual wealth, high ethical standards and perfect physical fitness must be harmoniously combined'.[5] An argument was put forward that the principal evils in the old society stemmed from the great gulf between manual and mental labour, and that the aim of a socialist society was to bring about a unity of physical and intellectual effort. This was to be achieved by combining instruction with productive work.

> To strengthen their ties with life the schools must not only introduce new subjects which teach the pupils the fundamentals of technology and production, but must also systematically accustom the pupils to working in factories, collective and state farms, experimental plots and school workshops.[6]

The Theses stressed that education in the schools must inculcate in children a love of knowledge and work, and a respect for people who work; it must shape the communist world outlook of the pupils and rear them in the spirit of communist morality and boundless loyalty to the country as well as in the spirit of proletarian internationalism. The higher education establishments were urged to produce people who had mastered their specialities well, who were active and passionate champions of Lenin's ideas and of the policy of the Communist Party and who were profoundly convinced of the ultimate triumph of the communist cause. The Soviet youth had to be brought up in a spirit of irreconcilability to bourgeois ideology and any manifestations of revisionism.

On 24 December 1958, within six weeks of the publication of the Theses, the law was passed on Strengthening the Ties of the School with Life and Further Development of the System of Public Education in the USSR. It repeated the arguments used by Khrushchev in his memorandum for introducing important changes in the system and resolved that:

1. universal and compulsory eight-year education shall be introduced in the USSR to replace universal and compulsory seven-year education;

2. complete secondary education of young people beginning from the age of fifteen or sixteen shall be carried out on the basis of combining study with productive work;

3. complete secondary education shall be given in three basic types of school: (a) schools for young workers and rural youth, offering part-time education in out-of-work hours, (b) secondary general education labour polytechnic schools with production training, offering three-year full-time education after eight years of compulsory general education, and (c) technical schools and other secondary specialised education establishments, offering both general secondary and specialised secondary education on a full-time and part-time basis;

4. production training and socially useful work may be carried out at instructional and production workshops in nearby industrial enterprises, in pupils' teams on collective and state farms, at instructional experimental farms and at instructional production workshops in schools or groups of schools.

Other articles specified the particular tasks facing teachers and students in vocational schools, specialised secondary education and higher education.

In August 1959 the Ministry of Education of the RSFSR issued new curricular plans for schools, to bring the changes envisaged by the 1958 law into operation. Humanist subjects came to occupy 39·5 per cent of the total teaching time, sciences

32·5 per cent, labour training and socially useful work 15·3 per cent, drawing, music and singing 6·2 per cent and physical education 6·5 per cent.[7]

The five-year basis of the economic plans was temporarily changed to a seven-year one in the late 1950s, but subsequently reverted to the original basis. The Twenty-first Congress of the CPSU in January 1959 set out the objectives for a Seven-Year Economic Plan (1959–65). These included the plans for progressive expansion of all the different branches of national life, economic as well as cultural.

Education during the Seventh and Eighth Five-Year Plans (1961–70)   The Twenty-second Congress of the CPSU in October 1961 adopted the Third Programme of the Communist Party of the USSR for the building of the communist society. Party programmes are important documents identifying long-term objectives; in 1919 the Second Party Programme had outlined the tasks for building a socialist society: the Third Party Programme did the same for the communist society of the future. In the field of public education the following were stated to be the main tasks facing the country in the period of transition to communism:

1. the solving of the 'cardinal social problem' of the elimination of substantial distinction between mental and physical labour;

2. the introduction of universal compulsory secondary education for all;

3. the public upbringing of children of pre-school age and school age in pre-school institutions and boarding schools of different types;

4. the creation of conditions for a high standard of instruction and education of the rising generation;

5. the expansion of higher and secondary specialised education.[8]

No specific time targets were set with respect to any of the above tasks, but, in general, the document dealt with the decades 1961–70 and 1971–80. According to the programme the creation of the material and technical basis for a communist society was to be accomplished by the end of the second decade.

The solution of the problem of bridging the gap between physical and mental work with the help of study combined with production training ran, however, into serious difficulties. The secondary general education labour polytechnic schools frequently could not cope in a satisfactory way with industrial practice and give students a wider range of choice of training, because of lack of the necessary resources, equipment and personnel. As a result, in August 1964, after five years' experience of implementing the reform of 1958, the Central Committee of the CPSU and the USSR Council of Ministers issued a decree concerning the Change of the Period of Instruction in Secondary General Education Labour Polytechnic Schools with Production Training; this shortened the length of studies in such schools from three to two years. Polytechnic education, practical training and courses in the theory and practice of production were, however, not abandoned, although the total time devoted to them was sharply reduced. The last graduation from the eleventh grade of secondary schools took place in 1966.

Another important decree, also issued in 1964, was one concerning the Periods of Training and the Improved Use of Specialists with Higher and Secondary Specialised Education. It cut the length of study in these fields by six to twelve months, depending upon speciality.

Little reference was made to education by Leonid Brezhnev in his Report of the Central Committee of the CPSU at the Twenty-third Party Congress in March 1966. He stressed the importance of education in the moulding of new communist man and in political, economic and cultural development, and called for a further improvement in the field. The directives of the Twenty-third Congress set before the country the task of completing the transition to universal secondary education by 1970.

In 1966 the federal Ministry of Education of the USSR was set up and the RSFSR Academy of Pedagogical Sciences was reorganised as the Academy of Pedagogical Sciences of the USSR. In the same year the Supreme Soviet established ten standing commissions under both Chambers for the basic spheres of economic, social and cultural development, including one on public education. Identical commissions were also formed in the Supreme Soviets of the Union republics. Also in 1966, a Scientific Methodological Council was set up under the Ministry of Higher and Secondary Specialised Education to improve teaching methods. Its members were prominent scientists, psychologists and teaching methods experts.

The 1966 Law on Polytechnic Education confirmed that the Soviet schools must develop on the basis of general education, labour training and polytechnic education. Labour training must involve the forming of correct attitudes to work, while polytechnic education must teach industrial skills as well as the principles of production. In the school year 1967/8 new syllabuses for labour training were introduced for all grades.

The 1967 Theses of the Central Committee of the CPSU on the Fiftieth Anniversary of the October Revolution identified the new and more complex tasks of communist education as the moulding of individuals in whom ideological steadfastness, love of work, discipline, spiritual wealth, moral purity and physical perfection would be harmoniously united. They repeatedly stressed the utmost importance of the training of specialists for the national economy, adding that this had to go hand in hand with the formation of noble ideals, communist ethics and respect for the rules of the socialist way of life: discipline and self-discipline, a thrifty attitude to public property, respect for others, a sense of human dignity and civic duty and an uncompromising attitude towards every manifestation of anti-social behaviour. In all, the Theses clearly formulated the central values of Soviet communist morality.

In August 1968 a law on the Expansion of Production of Visual Aids in Education and Educational Equipment announced the plans for an increased production of audiovisual aids for schools. In the same year a law on Universal Military Service introduced compulsory pre-conscription military training in all schools for boys aged fifteen and over.

The 1969 law on Shortening the Primary Phase of Education reduced the first cycle of education in the eight-year schools from four to three years. The decision was based upon long research by the Soviet scientists and psychologists N. A. Menchinskaya, D. B. Elkonin, L. V. Zankov, A. Lyublinskaya, S. M. Yazykov and the groups of research workers who were led by them. In the school year 1970/1 the first, second and fourth grades began their work according to the new syllabuses which condensed into three years the material formerly taught in the first four. New syllabuses were also introduced for a number of subjects in the higher grades.

In September 1970 the Statutes of the Secondary General Education Schools provided a unified and comprehensive collection of regulations for this type of school; these are discussed in the section on schools (see p 59).

Education and the Ninth Five-Year Plan (1971–5)   In the Report of the Central Committee of the CPSU, delivered to the Twenty-fourth Congress of the Party in March 1971, Leonid Brezhnev referred specifically to the task of introducing universal secondary education by 1970. He declared that, although the country was unable to reach this target, it did draw closer to it. About 80 per cent of pupils finishing eight-year schools went on to receive complete secondary education in 1970. Another directive of the Twenty-third Congress, on preparing 7 million specialists with higher or secondary specialised education over the course of the five years 1966–70, had been fulfilled.

In the Directives for the Five-Year Plan 1971–5 Alexei Kosygin declared the main task of the plan was to ensure a considerable rise in material and cultural standards by means of a high rate of development of socialist production, scientific and technical progress and a higher labour output. He stressed that the 1970 census of population showed that 75 per cent of the working population in towns and over 50 per cent in the country had a secondary or higher education. He promised universal secondary education by 1975 and the training of about 9 million specialists, including experts in new fields of science and technology, during the forthcoming five years. He declared that plans were being prepared to raise the salaries of schoolteachers and doctors throughout the country by 20 per cent, scholarship grants for students in higher education institutions by 25 per cent, and grants for students in secondary specialised educational establishments by an average of 50 per cent, all to take effect as from 1 September 1972.

According to the Soviet analysis of trends in educational development in the USSR, 19–20 per cent of all persons in the relevant age group should be receiving higher education in the Soviet Union in 1980, while the proportion of students receiving secondary specialised education should go up to between 28 and 30 per cent.[9]

THE SOCIO-POLITICAL SET-UP

It is difficult to interpret what has been happening or is happening, and to estimate what is likely to happen, to Soviet education without direct reference to the political background, that is, to the characteristic features of a society which for more than half a century has devoted all its efforts to the building of socialism and now sees itself as being in a stage of transition from socialism to communism.

According to the marxist-leninist theory socialism is based upon the principle of 'From each according to his ability, to each according to his work'. A definition of communism was given in the 1961 Programme of the Communist Party of the Soviet Union:

> Communism is a classless social system with one form of public ownership of the means of production and full social equality of all members of society; under it, the all-round development of people will be accompanied by the growth of the productive forces through continuous progress in science and technology; all the springs of co-operative wealth will flow more abundantly and the great principle 'From each according to his ability, to each according to his needs' will be implemented. Communism is a highly organised society of free, socially conscious working people in which public self-government will be established, a society in which labour for the good of society will become the prime vital requirement of everyone, a necessity recognised by one and all, and the ability of each person will be employed to the greatest benefit of the people.[10]

Marxist-leninist philosophy assumes a materialist world and

maintains that all forms of matter are in a state of constant development which proceeds according to objective laws, independent of man's volition or any supernatural force. According to Marx, 'the logic of the inexorable laws of social progress' makes for inevitable progression from capitalism to socialism and from socialism to communism.

The Communist Party of the Soviet Union   Politically, the significant point is that effective power in the USSR is in the hands of the only party, the Communist Party of the Soviet Union.

According to the Rules of the CPSU:

the Communist Party of the Soviet Union is the tried and tested militant vanguard of the Soviet people which unites, on a voluntary basis, the more advanced, politically more conscious section of the working class, collective farm peasantry and intelligentsia of the USSR.[11]

The membership of the CPSU was 12·6 million in 1967 and nearly 14·5 million in 1971. In the latter year 9 per cent of the entire adult population were Party members. Nearly 75 per cent of Party members work in industry, agriculture, transport, construction and trade; over 16 per cent work in the field of education, science, health and culture. More than half of the Party members are under forty years of age.

The supreme body of the Party is the Party Congress, convened in the past normally every four, and now every five, years. It is the Party Congress which hears and approves the reports of the Central Committee and determines the Party line in all matters of policy. Its decisions are binding on all Party organisations. Between Party Congresses the top Party body is the Central Committee, which selects and appoints the leading Party functionaries, sets up Party bodies and distributes Party funds. The numerical strength of the Central Committee may vary. The Twenty-third Congress elected 195 full members and 165 candidate members in 1966. The Central Committee elect the Politbureau and the Secretariat. The former directs the current work of the Party between the Central Committee plenums; the latter directs the current work, through its numerous sections.

The formal separation of the organs of state power in the USSR and the CPSU should be noted, but not misinterpreted. The highest organ of state power is the Supreme Soviet consisting of the Soviet of the Union and the Soviet of the Nationalities, elected by universal suffrage every four years. Its sessions take place, according to the Constitution, twice a year. The Supreme Soviet elects its Presidium which in the intervals between the sessions of the Supreme Soviet is the highest permanently functioning body of state power in the country. The real point is that almost all the members of the Presidium are members of the Central Committee of the CPSU or the Politbureau. In this way the formal separation of the CPSU and the state organs of power is for all practical purposes of little significance. On the other hand, the resolutions of the Party Congresses and the decisions of the Central Committee of the Party and the Politbureau are of utmost and direct significance for all policy measures.

The sole foundation upon which the CPSU bases all its policies is the ideology of marxism-leninism. Its theoretical components constitute marxist-leninist philosophy, based upon dialectical and historical materialism, political economy and so-called scientific communism. This is of great significance for political education in the institutions of higher learning.

The duties of the Party members and of the builders of communism The most important duties of a Party member are to take an active part in the political life of the country, in the administration of state affairs and in economic and cultural development; to set an example in the fulfilment of one's public duty; to assist in developing and strengthening communist social relations; to contribute to the moulding and education of communist man; to combat vigorously all manifestations of bourgeois ideology, religious prejudices and other survivals of the past, to implement undeviatingly the Party's policy and to observe Party and state discipline.[12]

The moral code of the builders of communism is said to incorporate the following ethical principles:

a. loyalty to the communist cause, love of the socialist motherland and the other socialist countries;

b. conscientious labour for the benefit of society;

c. concern for the protection and increase of public wealth;

d. collectivism and comradely mutual assistance;

e. humane relations and mutual respect among people;

f. honesty and truthfulness, moral purity, unpretentiousness and modesty in social and private life;

g. intolerance of injustice, parasitism, dishonesty, careerism and money-grubbing;

h. intolerance of the enemies of communism, the enemies of peace and those who oppose the freedom of nations;

i. fraternal solidarity with the working people of all countries, and with all peoples.[13]

Social differentiation   The 1970 census of population revealed that over a hundred different nationalities live in the Soviet Union. The largest group, the Russians, numbered then 129 million people; the smallest, the Yukaghiri, 600. Each different nationality is not confined to a particular union republic, autonomous republic or autonomous region, but often is represented in several administrative regions. In fact all the Union republics are multi-national. With the exception of Kazakhstan and Kirghizstan, the nationalities which have given names to the different republics constitute the majority of population there. As these majorities are, on the whole, in the region of 60–80 per cent, the minority groups are important in every republic.

The percentages of Russians living in the different Union republics varied considerably: from 83·3 per cent in the RSFSR, 42·7 in Kazakhstan, 30·2 in Kirghizstan, 26·6 in Latvia and 20·1 in Estonia, to 8·5 per cent in Lithuania, 8·2 in Byelorussia and 3·2 in Armenia in 1967.[14]

The cultural backgrounds of various nationalities differ considerably due to historical and racial influences. It is important to distinguish in this respect the Slavonic group (Russians, Ukrainians, Byelorussians), the Baltic nations (Lithuanians, Latvians, Estonians), the Caucasus peoples (Armenians and Georgians) and the Asiatic peoples (Kazakhs, Uzbeks, Kirghiz, Tadzhiks, Turkmen and other smaller nationalities).

The notions concerning the role of the family, the position of women in society and the attitudes towards life in general often still reflect in many areas the ideas and beliefs permeating the different cultures of the past.

It is very interesting that several more millions of people name Russian as their mother tongue than give their nationality as Russian. In the 1970 census 129 million declared themselves Russians; 141·8 million named Russian as their mother tongue, while 41·9 million said that Russian was their second language, of which they had a good command.[15]

Social stratification and urbanisation   The Soviet view is that there exist nowadays in the USSR only two social classes: the working class and the collective farmers. A considerable proportion of the total population constitute the intelligentsia, officially described as mental workers (*rabotniki umstvennogo truda*).

The official statistics with respect to social change indicate, through the course of the last sixty years since 1913, (1) a steady growth of manual and non-manual workers: 17 per cent of the population in 1913; 50·2 in 1939; 68·3 in 1959 and 78·4 in 1969; (2) a quick growth followed by gradual decline in the proportion of collective farmers and co-operative handicraftsmen: 2·9 per cent of the population in 1928; 47·2 in 1939; 31·4 in 1959 and 21·5 in 1969. The independent peasants and handicraftsmen, who in 1913 constituted 66·7 per cent of the population and 74·9 in 1928, have virtually ceased to exist, as, of course, have the bourgeoisie.[16]

The percentage of urban population has been increasing at a steady rate in the USSR, but particularly in the period 1950–60, when it increased from 39 to 49 per cent in the course of the decade. In 1970 it stood at 56 per cent. The crucial year in the process of change was 1962, when the urban population exceeded for the first time the rural population of the country.[17]

The study of the relationship between social class and education is only beginning to take place in the USSR and is very much in its first stages. Certain inquiries indicate that the opportunities for workers exceed those for collective farmers.[18]

The increasing proportion of urban population to rural is an

C

index of the growing concentration of population in larger, compact settlements, where educational opportunities tend to be superior to those in the rural areas, especially for full-time upper secondary and higher education.

The position of women   One of the more spectacular changes in the USSR has been in the role of women in Soviet society. From having been underprivileged and completely dependent upon their husbands, mostly illiterate and quite without prospects for independent professional life, they are now equal in status with men. Smaller families—due to the availability of contraceptives, widespread birth control and legalised abortions —have played a role in this process. Just as important has been the policy of providing equal educational opportunities for girls and throwing open to women many occupations and professions that are elsewhere still considered the prerogative of men. Particularly interesting is the provision of regular training for girls in vocational-technical education, leading to jobs in industry, transport and other services, in addition to the facilities permitting them to compete on equal terms with men for entry to the professions, as doctors, lawyers, scientists and engineers.

Regional differences, reflecting cultural values, still exist. Women constituted 50·5 per cent of all persons employed in the USSR in 1968, but the figure was 38 per cent for Tadzhikstan, 39 per cent for Turkmenistan and 40 per cent for Uzbekistan and Azerbaidzhan.[19]

DEMOGRAPHIC CHANGES

Demographic changes, in particular the changes in population growth, birth rate and migration, have an important effect on the extent and quality of educational provision.

Population growth   The general rate of growth of population in the USSR has slowed down in recent years. The country's population increased by 34 million people in the decade 1950–60, and only by 30 million in the decade 1960–70. The rate of natural increase showed, however, great differences between the individual Union republics. In 1969 it exceeded 20 per 1,000 of population in the Central Asiatic republics (Uzbekistan, Azerbaidzhan,

Kirghizstan, Tadzhikstan and Turkmenistan), but was well below 10 per 1,000 in the RSFSR, the Ukraine, Byelorussia, Lithuania, Latvia and Estonia.[20]

Table 1

Territory, Population, Population Density and Proportion of Urban Population of the Union Republics (15 January 1970)

	Territory in 000 sq km	Total population in 000	Population density per sq km	Proportion of urban population
USSR	22,402·2	241,748	10·9	56
RSFSR	17,075·4	130,090	7·6	62
Ukraine	603·7	47,136	78·1	55
Byelorussia	207·6	9,003	43·4	43
Uzbekistan	449·6	11,963	26·6	36
Kazakhstan	2,715·1	12,850	4·7	51
Georgia	69·7	4,688	67·3	48
Azerbaidzhan	86·6	5,111	59·0	50
Lithuania	65·2	3,129	48·0	50
Moldavia	33·7	3,572	106·0	32
Latvia	63·7	2,365	37·1	62
Kirghizstan	198·5	2,933	14·8	37
Tadzhikstan	143·1	2,900	20·3	37
Armenia	29·8	2,493	83·7	59
Turkmenistan	488·1	2,158	4·4	48
Estonia	45·1	1,357	30·1	65

Source: Tsentralnoe Statisticheskoe Upravlenie. *Narodnoe khozyaystvo SSSR v 1969 g.* (Moscow 1970), 9, 11, 13–18.

The changes in the rate of growth of the populations of the different Union republics are now, however, identical with the changes in the size of the different ethnic groups, as each republic consists of a number of nationalities. Between 1959 and 1970 the number of Russians rose from 114 million to 129 million; Ukrainians from 37·3 to 40·8 million; Uzbeks from 6·0 to 9·2 million; Byelorussians from 7·9 to 9·1 million; Tartars from 5·0 to 5·9 million; Kazakhs from 3·6 to 5·3 million; Azerbaidzhanis from 2·9 to 4·4 million; Armenians from 2·8 to 3·6 million. The rate of growth of the different nationalities is very uneven, the highest being for those in Soviet Asia and the lowest for those in the Baltic areas.[21]

On 15 January 1970 the Soviet Union had a total population of 241,720,000 people of whom 111,399,000 were males and 130,321,000 were females. The disproportion between the sexes is due to enormous war losses among men. In 1959 there were 819 and in 1970 855 men per 1,000 women; as time goes on the gap between the number of men and the number of women narrows, and in any case it does not apply to the younger section of the population under forty in 1970.[22]

Birth rate   Table 2 shows that there has been a pronounced and consistent tendency towards a lower birth rate in the USSR over the last fifty years or so.

Table 2

Birth Rate in the USSR (1913–69)
(number of births per 1,000 of population)

Year	Birth Rate	Year	Birth Rate
1913	47·0	1960	24·9
1926	44·0	1961	23·8
1937	38·7	1962	22·4
1940	31·2	1963	21·1
1950	26·7	1964	19·5
1955	25·7	1965	18·4
1956	25·2	1966	18·2
1957	25·4	1967	17·3
1958	25·3	1968	17·2
1959	25·0	1969	17·0

Source: Tsentralnoe Statisticheskoe Upravlenie. *Narodnoe khozyaystvo SSSR v 1969 g.* (Moscow 1970), 31.

Significantly, the differential birth rates in the USSR show great divergencies which can be seen from Table 3.

Due to the decline in the overall birth rate in the USSR in recent years, the proportion of young children in the population has decreased. In 1970 children under four years of age accounted for 8·5 per cent of the population, while in 1959 they constituted 11·7 per cent.[23]

From the absolute figures of the number of infants born in the Soviet Union in the decade 1960–70 it is clear that the country has been and will be providing school places for fewer and fewer children starting school at seven, for at least several years from

Table 3

Birth Rates, Death Rates and Rates of Natural Increase of Population in the Union Republics (1969)

(per 1,000 of population)

Union Republic	Birth Rate	Death Rate	Rate of increase of population
RSFSR	14·2	8·5	5·7
Ukraine	14·6	8·6	6·0
Byelorussia	15·9	7·4	8·5
Uzbekistan	32·7	5·9	26·8
Kazakhstan	23·5	6·2	17·3
Georgia	18·7	7·5	11·2
Azerbaidzhan	29·3	7·0	22·3
Lithuania	17·4	8·7	8·7
Moldavia	18·9	7·4	11·5
Latvia	14·0	11·1	2·9
Kirghizstan	30·1	7·5	22·6
Tadzhikstan	34·7	6·1	28·6
Armenia	22·8	5·2	17·6
Turkmenistan	34·3	7·0	27·3
Estonia	15·5	11·3	4·2

Source: Tsentralnoe Statisticheskoe Upravlenie. *Narodnoe khozyaystvo SSSR v 1969 g.* (Moscow 1970), 34–5.

1967. However, as the number of pupils in the compulsory sector of education is bound to decline somewhat, more and more places have to be provided in the post-compulsory sector, due to the increasing number of adolescents staying on at school after the age of fifteen.

Internal migration   Internal migration is another factor influencing educational developments. In the period 1959–67 the territories with considerable excess of arrivals over departures were: Kazakhstan (over 1 million), North Caucasus (over 760,000), the Ukraine, Uzbekistan, the Far East, Kirghizstan, Tadzhikstan, Latvia (all over 100,000), Moldavia, Armenia, Estonia, Lithuania, Turkmenistan and the north-western area of the RSFSR (up to 100,000). The territories with excess of departures over arrivals were: the Volgo-Vyatsk area (845,000), the Central area, the Ural area, the Central Black Earth area, Western Siberia, Byelorussia and Eastern Siberia (all over 100,000). In some regions, notably in the Volgo-Vyatsk area, the migration outflow of population even exceeded the natural increase in this period, so that population actually declined there.[24]

In general, the demographic trends and the economic and social development of the country constitute the background influences which are no less important for educational growth and change in the USSR than the impact of ideology and political considerations.

Notes to chapter 1 are on pp 126–7

2

Administration, Finance and Planning

ADMINISTRATION OF EDUCATION

Constitutional basis of educational organisation Article 14 of the Constitution of 5 December 1936 lists the jurisdiction reserved for the Union. Paragraph t of this Article contains a direct reference to the authority of the Union in 'establishment of the basic principles in the sphere of education'.

Article 121, included in Chapter X on Fundamental Rights and Duties of Citizens, lays down the principle of the right to education and lists the specific measures designed to ensure this right:

> The citizens of the USSR have the right to an education. This right is ensured by the compulsory general schooling of eight years; by the wide development of general and polytechnical secondary education, of vocational and technical training and of higher and specialised secondary education on the basis of joint development of education, life and production; by the development of evening and correspondence courses; by the gratuity of all forms of education; by the system of state scholarships, free education in the mother tongue in the schools and the organisation of free vocational, technical and agricultural instruction for the workers in factories, state and collective farms.[1]

The general principles of administration of education The entire system of public education in the USSR is directed and administered by government departments. There is no private sector.

The Supreme Soviet of the USSR is responsible for laying down the basic principles in the field of education in the shape of laws. Legislation on education in the Union republics and autonomous republics is enacted by the Supreme Soviets of these republics.

The laws on education issued by the Supreme Soviet of the USSR are binding for a Union republic, and the laws of the USSR and a Union republic are binding for an autonomous republic.

The supreme executive and administrative organ of state authority in the field of education is the Council of Ministers of the USSR which issues rules and regulations on educational matters on the basis and in implementation of the existing All-Union laws. In the Union republics and autonomous republics these functions are exercised by the Councils of Ministers of those republics.

The Councils of Ministers of the USSR, the Union republics and the autonomous republics administer education through the corresponding Ministries of Education. In the USSR there exist three types of ministry: All-Union, Union-republican and re-public. Each All-Union ministry exercises direct and sole control over the whole Soviet Union. Union-republican ministries exercise control through the corresponding ministries within the republics. Republic ministries are state organs of power administering matters in a given field within each of the fifteen republics.

At the present time the management of education in the USSR is effected by three channels:

1. pre-school education, general education and the development of the pedagogical sciences in the country are under the Ministry of Education of the USSR;

2. secondary specialised and higher education are under the Ministry of Higher and Secondary Specialised Education of the USSR;

3. vocational-technical education is under the State Committee of the Council of Ministers of the USSR for Vocational-Technical Education.

Ministry of Education of the USSR   Pre-school and general school education was up to 1966 administered by the Ministries of Education of the Union republics and autonomous republics. In 1966 the Union-republican Ministry of Education of the USSR was set up because of the need for a greater synchronisation of effort in tackling the national problems in a uniform way and securing proper co-ordination in research and development. The explicit duties of the Ministry of Education of the USSR include the following:

a. ensuring communist education of children and youth, and providing for their spiritual, physical and aesthetic development;

b. management of pre-school education, primary and secondary general education and out-of-school education;

c. promotion and co-ordination of pedagogical science and research in the country;

d. elaboration and carrying out of measures on the further development and improvement of the system of people's education and presenting the corresponding proposals for the consideration of the government;

e. specification of targets for the current and long-term educational plans in collaboration with the Councils of Ministers of the republics;

f. determination of the content of general secondary polytechnic education and labour training of the pupils;

g. improvement of the educational curricula for secondary schools of general education;

h. preparation and publishing of school textbooks;

i. rendering assistance to the republics of the Union in improving the management of schools and pre-school and out-of-school educational establishments;

j. fostering improvement in the professional skills of teachers and other workers in education;

k. development of foreign relations in the field of education.[2]

In order to give proper consideration, in the plans for general development of schools in the country, to the educational features peculiar to the particular republics, a Council for the Problems of Secondary Schools of General Education has been established at the Ministry of Education of the USSR. It includes the Minister, Deputy Ministers, the President of the Academy of Pedagogical Sciences of the USSR and the Ministers of Education of all Union republics. The function of the Council is to give consideration to all important problems in education and to draft plans of development and school regulations; to determine school curricula and programmes; to examine the development of the pedagogical sciences and to ensure co-ordination of the work of research institutions.

A Board of Authorities has also been set up at the Ministry consisting of the Minister who acts as the chairman, Deputy Ministers, a small number of the Ministry's officials and the President of the Academy of Pedagogical Sciences of the USSR. At its regular meetings the Board considers the problems of development of education and pedagogical sciences, as well as the questions of practical management of the educational institutions and establishments, and receives reports from the authorities responsible for it.

The Ministry's Scientific Council on Methods of Teaching considers and decides the issues concerning changes in school curricula, textbooks, teaching aids and teaching methods, and works out recommendations on the utilisation of the results of pedagogical research. It consists of outstanding scientists, highly skilled specialists and representatives of the scientific pedagogical societies and similar institutions.

The Academy of Pedagogical Sciences (*Akademiya Pedagogicheskikh Nauk*)   The Academy of Pedagogical Sciences of the RSFSR was founded on 6 October 1943. In 1966, when the Ministry of Education of the USSR was created, it became the Academy of the Pedagogical Sciences of the USSR.

Its first president was Academician Vladimir Potemkin; its second Professor I. A. Kairov; its third Professor V. M. Khvostov and its fourth is Professor V. N. Stoletov. The former vice-presidents included Professor N. K. Goncharov, Professor A. A. Smirnov and Professor A. Leontiev. The present vice-presidents are Professor A. I. Markushevich, Professor V. G. Zubov and Professor A. G. Khripkova. In 1970 the members of the Presidium, in addition to the president and the vice-presidents, were Professors N. P. Kuzin, A. V. Zaporozhets, I. A. Kairov, F. F. Karolev, G. S. Kostyuk and M. A. Prokofiev.

The Academy consists of a body of members and corresponding members, who are all distinguished scientists working in the different fields of pedagogical science. New members are elected by the existing members from the ranks of outstanding scientists. The total membership in March 1970 was 126, of whom 48 were full members and 78 corresponding members. Both categories are entitled to the rank of Academician.

The Academy is made up of a number of institutes and pedagogical laboratories. The following were the institutes of the Academy in 1970:

Institute of Theory and History of Education
Institute of General and Polytechnic Education
Institute of General and Educational Psychology
Institute of Developmental Psychology
Institute of Pre-school Education
Institute of Physical Education and School Hygiene
Institute of Aesthetic Education
Institute of Industrial and Vocational Training
Institute of Didactics and Teaching Methods
Institute of Defectology
Institute of National Schools
Institute of Adult Education

The Institutes are divided into departments, specialising in particular aspects of educational development or pedagogy (eg, the Department of Moral Education and Character Training in the Institute of Theory and History of Education). They are supported, financed and controlled by the Academy. Under the Academy also are the famous Ushinsky State Library on Education with its 1 million volumes, the Educational Research Archives and the National Education Museum in Leningrad.

The fundamental aim of the Academy is a thorough examination of the problems of education and educational development from the scientific point of view, the promotion of training of scientific personnel in pedagogic sciences, and the dissemination of pedagogic knowledge among the people. The research work is conducted by Institutes' members in the pedagogic laboratories, which included in 1970 8 experimental schools, 2 boarding schools, 2 specialised boarding schools and 127 other schools. The research work varies in quality and is directed towards the solution of current problems in education. Outstanding results have, however, been achieved in the field of psychology under the guidance of distinguished Soviet psychologists: Professor Anatoly Smirnov, Professor Aleksei Leontiev, Professor A. R. Luria and Professor A. V. Zaporozhets.

The Academy's publishing house regularly issues important pedagogical periodicals: *Sovetskaya Pedagogika* (Soviet Pedagogy), *Semya i Shkola* (Family and School), *Voprosy Psikhologii* (Problems of Psychology) and *Russkii Yazyk v Natsionalnoy Shkole* (Russian Language in the National School) and two well-known series of reports on current research: *Izvestia APN* (Academy's News) and *Novye Issledovaniya v Pedagogicheskikh Naukakh* (New Research in the Pedagogical Sciences). In 1960 the Academy published the two volumes of *Pedagogicheskii Slovar* (Pedagogical Dictionary). Reprints of important books on educational theory include the works of K. D. Ushinsky, A. I. Herzen, V. G. Belinsky, N. G. Chernyshevsky, N. A. Dobrolyubov, L. N. Tolstoy, N. K. Krupskaya, M. N. Kalinin and A. S. Makarenko.

The Academy also awards every year the Konstantin Ushinsky Prize for an outstanding book in the fields of pedagogy or education.[3]

Ministries of Education of the Union republics and local administration of education   The Ministries of Education of the fifteen Union republics make plans for developing the network of pre-school institutions, schools, pedagogic schools and out-of-school educational establishments in their areas. They are responsible for the general direction of education, draw up regulations concerning school education and school work and supply and maintain school equipment. They guide and control the regional and local organs of education. The autonomous republics have their own Ministries of Education.

Direct control of the work of pre-school institutions and schools is exercised by the district and municipal departments of education. They have jurisdiction over the directors of schools in their areas. They also maintain their own staff of inspectors of schools, each inspector being assigned to a number of schools. The inspector's duty is to visit each school at least twice during the year and check on the proficiency of the director and the teaching staff and, in particular, that the laws, rules and regulations are observed and the instructions are implemented. The departments of education are responsible to the executive committees of local soviets.

The Ministry of Higher and Secondary Specialised Education of the USSR The Ministry of Higher and Secondary Specialised Education of the USSR exercises overall supervision of all the higher education establishments which include the universities and the polytechnic and specialised institutes as well as the secondary specialised education establishments. The Ministry is generally responsible for the unity of the pedagogical process. In particular it is responsible for the following:

a. establishment of the conditions for admission of students to all institutions of higher and secondary specialised education;

b. preparation and approval of curricula in such institutions;

c. establishment of methods of recruitment of the teaching staff;

d. preparation of the lists of specialities taught in such institutions;

e. methodological directives concerning the organisation of instruction;

f. supervision of the organisation of instruction leading to scientific research and higher degrees;

g. publication of a large proportion of the textbooks used in higher education;

h. study of building plans for universities and institutions of equivalent rank through a specialised agency under the Ministry known as the *Giprovuz*.[4]

It was decided in 1966 that the Ministry of Higher and Specialised Secondary Education of the USSR should inspect higher education establishments in the country. As the first step in this direction a number of universities and major institutes of higher education were placed under the Ministry's direct control as a testing ground for research and methodological work. Other institutes have been left to carry on under the republican Ministries of Higher and Secondary Specialised Education (in

Azerbaidzhan, Armenia, Georgia, Lithuania and Estonia under republican state committees) or other ministries.[5]

Ministries of Higher and Secondary Specialised Education of the Union republics   The administration and finance of the majority of higher education establishments are the responsibility of the Union republics. Each republic has either a republican Ministry of Higher and Secondary Specialised Education or a committee to administer such establishments. The following institutions fall into this category: universities, polytechnic institutes specialising in industry, power, electro-technology, radio-technology, physics-technology, machine building, instrument making, shipbuilding, aviation, machine-tool making, mechanics, geology, chemical technology, food technology, fishing industry, textiles, building, geodesy, economics, law and architecture.

Some of the specialised institutes are, on the other hand, subordinated to other ministries; for example, higher education establishments in agriculture, transport and communications come under the corresponding ministries; the medical ones, under the Ministry of Public Health; those in art and trade come under the Ministries of Culture and Trade respectively.

The republican authorities are responsible for questions of finance, admission of new students, co-ordination of teaching and research and the preparation of scientific personnel.

The secondary specialised education establishments are generally subordinated to the Union republic Ministries of Higher and Secondary Specialised Education or other ministries in much the same way as the institutions of higher education, depending upon their specialisation. They are, however, opened, reorganised or closed only by agreement with the Ministry of Higher and Secondary Specialised Education of the USSR and the USSR Ministry of Finance.

The State Committee of the USSR Council of Ministers for Vocational-Technical Education   The State Committee of the USSR Council of Ministers for Vocational-Technical Education controls and guides the work of all vocational-technical schools in the country. It works out standard curricula for each trade or specialisation and it determines the number of students to be trained in each field, in close co-operation with the state planning authorities. The Council of Ministers of each Union republic must present its estimates of additional requirements in its skilled labour force annually to the USSR Council of Ministers and *Gosplan* (see p 51). The estimates cover all enterprises, institutions and organisations situated in the republic, irrespective of which administration controls them. They are added up to give an overall figure for the additional requirements in skilled workers according to specialisation. This serves in turn as the basis for drawing up the final plans for specialist training in vocational-technical schools, or direct training in industry.

Administration of education in the USSR—summary

Level of government administration	Pre-school establishments, primary and secondary general education schools	Vocational-technical establishments	Secondary specialised and higher education establishments
Union	Ministry of Education of the USSR	State Committee of the USSR Council of Ministers for Vocational and Technical Education	Ministry of Higher and Secondary Specialised Education
Union Republic	Union Republic Ministry of Education	State Committee of the Council of Ministers of the Union Republic for Vocational and Technical Education	Union Republic Ministry of Higher and Secondary Specialised Education

| Region (*Oblast*) or City (*Gorod*) | Regional or City Department of Education | Regional or City Committee for Vocational and Technical Education | — |
| District (*Raion*) | District Department of Education | — | — |

FINANCING OF EDUCATION

Sources of funds for education   The monetary expenditure on education in the Soviet Union comes basically from the state budget, chiefly at the Union, republican and local levels, and only to a very limited extent from the contributions of the state, co-operative, trade union and other public enterprises and organisations. The relative proportions in terms of absolute figures can be seen from Table 4.

Table 4

Sources of funds of Expenditure on Education
(in millions of roubles)

Source	1960	1964
Union budget	362	622
Republican budget	2,543	3,277
Local budget	4,938	6,984
Receipts from parents*	393	690
Social security	76	112
Trade unions	10	14
State economic organisations	61	27
Total	8,383	11,726

* Parental contributions for the maintenance of their children in crèches, kindergartens, pioneer camps and boarding schools.

Source: Unesco International Institute for Educational Planning, *Educational Planning in the USSR* (Paris 1969), 164.

It is important to remember that the main sources of revenue in the Soviet Union for budgetary expenditure are the accumulations of industrial, agricultural, transport, trading and other enterprises which in all account for more than 90 per cent of the entire revenue.

Expenditure on education   In the case of schools of general education the budgetary appropriations are calculated by the district, city or regional departments of education and by the Ministries of Education of the autonomous and Union republics on the basis of estimates of expenditure forwarded annually by all educational establishments and submitted to the Ministries of Finance of the corresponding republics.

In the case of vocational-technical schools they are calculated by the State Committee of the Council of Ministers of the USSR for Vocational-Technical Education and submitted to the USSR Ministry of Finance.

In the case of secondary specialised and higher education establishments they are calculated by the USSR and Union republic ministries and departments to which they are subordinated, and submitted to the Ministry of Finance of the USSR or of the Union republics concerned.

The details of the distribution of educational expenditure are given in Table 5.

Table 5

Distribution of Expenditure on Education from the State Budget
(in millions of roubles)

	1965	1969
Pre-school education	1,695	2,495
Children's homes, boarding and special schools	363	401
General education schools of all types	5,710	6,652
Cultural-educational work	424	653
Higher education establishments	1,483	2,070
Secondary specialised education establishments	829	1,164
Vocational-technical establishments	840	1,226
Press, arts and broadcasting	390	694
Capital expenditure	866	1,115
Other expenditure	645	955
Total	13,245	17,425

Source: Tsentralnoe Statisticheskoe Upravlenie. *Narodnoe khozyaystvo SSSR v 1969 g.* (Moscow 1970), 772.

D

After the state budget has been approved by the USSR Council of Ministers and the Supreme Soviet of the USSR, the expenditure estimates for each educational establishment are approved at the appropriate levels. Of the USSR state expenditure on secondary specialised education about 35 per cent is spent on the salaries of the teaching staff and other workers and about 30 per cent on students' grants. In higher education the corresponding figures are about 45 and 30 per cent.[6]

Because the basic financing of educational institutions is highly centralised and the funds are provided by the single state budget, there is a basic equality of educational provision throughout the country. The system acts, therefore, as a mechanism tending to equalise educational development in all the different regions of the USSR.

Average costs per student   The average costs per pupil or per student have been assessed in different ways. According to the inquiry by the mission of the International Institute for Educational Planning in Paris which visited the USSR in 1964, the average cost per pupil per annum in day nurseries and kindergartens was 410 roubles and in general education schools 99 roubles (see note on foreign currency equivalents, p 10); the cost per student in vocational-technical schools was 413 roubles, in secondary specialised education establishments 191 roubles and in higher education institutions 351 roubles. The costs of alternative types of instruction in 1959 in secondary specialised education were: day students—447 roubles; evening students—111 roubles; correspondence students—52 roubles. In higher education they were: day students—1,058 roubles; evening students—290 roubles; correspondence students—81 roubles.[7]

The percentage of the GNP devoted to education in the USSR has been estimated as between 5·3 and 5·4 per cent in 1964, and at that time it very much exceeded the corresponding figures for other industrialised countries.[8]

EDUCATIONAL PLANNING

Planning the development of the national economy has been one of the most characteristic features of Soviet economic policy since the late 1920s. Manpower planning necessitated the preparation of adequate numbers of skilled workers, technicians and technologists in the different specialisations. For this reason educational planning had to be closely integrated with economic planning, particularly at the levels of vocational-technical, secondary specialised and higher education. This has played an important role over the last four decades.

Proposals for the development of secondary general, vocational, secondary specialised and higher education are prepared by the individual educational establishments, government departments, ministries, Party, Trade Union and Komsomol organisations on the basis of the general objectives set out by the USSR State Planning Commission (*Gosplan*). These are formulated in quantitative terms by *Gosplan* authorities on the basis of the programme of the CPSU, the directives of the Central Committee of the Party and the decisions of the Council of Ministers. With the assistance and participation of the Union republics, the ministries and departments of the USSR, *Gosplan* divisions draft annual and long-term plans of development for all branches of the economy including education.

The Gosplan Division of Culture and Education   The *Gosplan* Division of Culture and Education first provides for the discussion of the draft plans for educational development in the Union republic *Gosplans* as well as in the USSR *Gosplan*. Directly involved are the ministries and departments in charge of educational establishments: the Ministries of Education and of Higher and Secondary Specialised Education of the USSR, the corresponding ministries and committees at the republic level, the State Committee for Vocational-Technical Education as well as the ministries utilising skilled workers of all kinds, the Ministry of Finance of the USSR, the State Committee of the Council of Ministers of the USSR on Labour and Wages, the Academy of Sciences of the USSR and other institutions.

The *Gosplan* Division of Culture and Education comprises the subdivisions of culture and the three following subdivisions: (1) of education, planning the development of all types of schools of general education and pre-school establishments; (2) for the training and re-assignment of specialists, concerned with planning development in the fields of higher and secondary specialised education; and (3) of labour, productivity, wages and labour resources, which plans the training of skilled workers in the vocational-technical schools.

The Division plays an important role by analysing in detail all draft plans submitted to it by the Union republics, ministries, departments and other agencies, from the point of view both of the technical and economic validity of the drafts. It then itself prepares a draft outlining the development of education and culture, both within the framework of the country as a whole and within each Union republic and each ministry involved.

The contents of the draft plan include the following major items:

a. the specification of the numbers of schools and pupils in the different types of school, and the specification of the numbers of students to be admitted and trained in vocational-technical schools, secondary specialised and higher education establishments;

b. the number of personnel employed in educational institutions of all kinds;

c. the volume of investment required for expanding education, including construction plans and finance;

d. the finances necessary for the maintenance of the existing educational institutions which are to be included in the state budget.[9]

For the purpose of determining the exact nature of the different kinds of specialisation at the levels of secondary specialised, vocational-technical and higher education, very detailed lists of specialisations, which include several thousands of entries, have been elaborated by *Gosplan*.

The co-ordination of draft plans   The draft plans prepared by the different branches of *Gosplan* have to be synchronised and co-ordinated in the Balance and General Divisions of *Gosplan*. Individual branches have to defend their drafts and proposals against the claims of other branches. This is a crucial stage at which the various demands must be tailored to match the resources available. When the final agreement is reached, the USSR *Gosplan* authorities present the overall draft plan to the Council of Ministers of the USSR as a single programme of development for the next year or the next five-year period. This includes a report on the draft plan, explaining the basic goals and targets with regard to the economy as a whole; the draft plan itself, with details concerning each branch; and also a specification of the objectives for each year, including a statistical analysis.

The USSR Council of Ministers discusses the draft plan with scientists, economic planners and experts and, after approval, submits the long-term plans for consideration to the Control Committee of the CPSU and the current plans to the Supreme Soviet of the USSR. The former are considered and accepted at the Congresses of the CPSU which issue directives on the development plan for the relevant period. The short-term current plans are considered by the Economic Committee of the Soviet of Nationalities and the Budget Committees of the Soviet of the Union and of the Soviet of Nationalities. Every year the Supreme Soviet of the USSR enacts legislation on the state plan for economic development, including educational development, and on the USSR state budget for the next planning year.[10]

Notes to chapter 2 are on p 127

3
The School System

PRE-SCHOOL EDUCATION

PRE-SCHOOL education, although neither free nor compulsory, constitutes an important part of the general system of education in the USSR. There exist a number of different kinds of institution at this level.

Nurseries (*Yasli*)   Nurseries accept children from six months, or even younger on occasions, to three years and are run by the different enterprises for the benefit of their own workers or by the Ministry of Health. Generally, they operate on a permanent basis, but there are also seasonal nurseries operating in the rural areas.

There is no set programme for the nurseries. The children are divided into small groups (usually of about fifteen to twenty) according to age, and are cared for by two qualified nurses and their assistants. The time is spent in playing, individually with toys or in groups, taking the meals provided and resting. Medical care is given and records are kept to maintain a proper check on the children's growth, weight and health. Children are normally brought to the nursery every morning and collected late in the afternoon or early in the evening, but some nurseries operate on a twenty-four-hour basis.

Kindergartens (*Detskie sady*) **and nursery-kindergartens** (*Yasli-sady*)   The kindergartens accept children from three to seven years of age. There also exist nowadays many combined nurseries and kindergartens, taking children from the age of a few months to seven years. Some are permanent, whole-day, whole-year institutions; some are seasonal establishments, open in the rural areas in the summer. In the urban areas there are also children's playgrounds, while special kindergarten-sanatoria accept children in need of special medical care. According to the official statistics, in 1969 7,835,200 children attended the permanent kindergartens and nursery-kindergartens, while over 4,000,000 attended the seasonal establishments.

The large conurbations of Moscow, Leningrad, Kiev, Baku, Kharkov, Tashkent, Gorky, Novosibirsk, Kuibyshev and Sverdlovsk possess pre-school facilities adequate for 50–80 per cent of the children in this age group, while the smaller settlements and the rural areas still lag behind, although in the decade 1960–70 the collective farms have built nurseries and kindergartens for 1·2 million children. It is estimated that to meet fully the demand for pre-school education, around 12 million places are necessary. According to the official estimates this should be achieved by 1975.[1]

The gradual growth of pre-school opportunities from 1927 to the present day can be seen from the accompanying table.

Table 6

Number of Kindergartens, Nursery-Kindergartens, their Children and Teachers

Year	Number of kindergartens and nursery-kindergartens	Number of children			Number of teachers (000)
		Urban areas (000)	Rural areas (000)	Total (000)	
1927	2,100	99·1	8·4	107·5	6·1
1932	19,600	710·2	351·5	1,061·7	52·0
1937	24,500	697·6	347·7	1,045·3	71·5
1940	24,000	905·4	266·1	1,171·5	75·2
1945	28,400	1,113·6	357·4	1,471·0	101·3
1950	25,600	958·1	210·7	1,168·8	92·6
1960	43,600	2,550·3	564·8	3,115·1	243·4
1965	67,500	5,000·4	1,206·9	6,207·3	453·3
1968	78,300	6,043·0	1,494·0	7,537·0	536·0
1969	80,700	6,227·4	1,607·8	7,835·2	557·7

Source: Tsentralnoe Statisticheskoe Upravlenie. *Narodnoe khozyaystvo SSSR v 1969 g.* (Moscow 1970), 672–3.

The pre-school establishments provide extensive opportunities for young mothers to carry on with full-time employment. Their aims are to introduce the children to the experience of collective life, to prepare them for school by supplying them with the elements of knowledge appropriate for their age and instilling in them a sense of discipline and the basic social skills and habits commensurate with the spirit of communist morality.

Currently, it is not envisaged that all the parents will ever want to have their children educated in the pre-school establishments; the role of the family in the upbringing of the Soviet children is not expected to decline:

> An extensive development of the network of pre-school institutions, a strict scientific organisation of the collective education of children and successful achievements to this end in no way reduce the role of the family in the education of children. The family is and remains the most important cell of society where a future citizen is moulded.[2]

Most kindergartens and nursery-kindergartens are state institutions, but a number have been built on the initiative and with the financial support of collective farms and industrial enterprises. The cost of maintenance of a child in a kindergarten is around 410 roubles per annum. Parents pay for the education of their children according to their ability to pay.

The children, after arrival and breakfast, have play and learning periods and an outside walk in the morning. After lunch they rest and play, have an afternoon snack and, sometimes, supper also before they go home. The aim of the learning periods is to acquaint the older children through the help of games with the letters of the alphabet and certain combinations of letters, as well as with simple counting, to enable them to express themselves clearly and to teach them the names of the different objects they come into contact with during the day. Particular attention is given to physical exercises and personal hygiene. Other aspects of education which are looked on as important are moral education, artistic-creative activities and the fostering of simple working habits.

Kindergarten teachers are trained in special faculties at pedagogic institutes or at pedagogic schools. Pre-school education is

given considerable attention in the research work of Soviet pedagogues. In November 1960 the Institute of Pre-school Education
was created as an important establishment in the Academy of
Pedagogical Sciences, to provide an opportunity for co-ordinated
research by psychologists, educators, doctors and physiologists
into the problems of pre-school education and the intellectual and
physical development of very young children. In recent years
particular stress was put on the study of the importance of play
(D. V. Mendzheridska, R. I. Zhukovska, A. V. Cherkovy), the
psychological aspects of growth (A. N. Leontiev, D. B. Elkonin),
concept formation and the thinking process (A. V. Zaporozhets,
P. Ya. Galperin, N. I. Nepomnyashchaya, G. P. Shchedrovitsky,
G. S. Kostyuk), aesthetic education (N. P. Sakulina, N. A.
Betlugina) and physical education (I. G. Levi-Gorinevskaya,
A. I. Bykov, T. I. Osokin, M. A. Sorochek, R. G. Uvarov).

UNIVERSAL COMPULSORY EDUCATION

Universal general full-time education is compulsory for all children from the age of seven to fifteen and covers the primary and
lower secondary stages of education. It includes the following
kinds of school:

1. primary schools consisting of the first four (in future the
first three, see p 27) grades;

2. incomplete secondary schools (eight-year schools) consisting of grades one to eight;

3. the first eight grades of the complete secondary schools
(ten-year schools consisting of grades one to ten).

Compulsory education is not coterminous with general education. General education covers, in fact, the primary grades and
the lower secondary grades for all children, as well as the upper
secondary grades (nine and ten) in secondary general education
schools for some children.

The situation is, however, complicated by the fact that the
Soviet laws and regulations on general secondary schools refer, in
fact, to all grades from one to ten and apply to primary schools,
eight-year schools and ten-year schools. It is, none the less,
important to remember that the fundamental unity of education

and the formal equality of educational opportunity is based upon uniform, undifferentiated, compulsory, free and secular education for all children from seven to fifteen.

Primary schools (*Nachalnye shkoly*)   Primary schools (grade one to grade four, and in future grades one to three inclusive) exist in the rural areas and will continue to exist in the sparsely populated areas. The process of rationalisation of the school network makes, however, for the gradual closing down of small-size primary schools as separate entities. The extent of it can be seen from Table 7. According to the letter of the law the authorities must provide a separate primary school in any place where there are not fewer than fifteen children of school age and where the nearest school is over a mile away.

Table 7

Primary, Incomplete Secondary and Complete Secondary Schools
(at the beginning of the school year)

	1940/41	1950/51	1960/61	1965/66	1969/70
Number of schools					
(in 000)	191·5	201·6	199·2	190·4	180·1
including					
primary schools	125·9	126·4	110·1	94·4	80·8
incomplete secondary schools	45·7	59·6	58·9	62·4	54·4
complete secondary schools	18·8	15·0	29·2	31·9	42·9
schools for mentally and physically handicapped	1·1	0·6	1·0	1·7	2·0
Number of pupils					
(in millions)	34·8	33·3	33·4	43·4	45·4
including those in					
primary schools	9·8	7·5	4·4	3·8	3·1
incomplete secondary schools	12·5	15·5	12·0	16·6	12·8
complete secondary schools	12·2	10·2	16·9	22·7	29·2
schools for mentally and physically handicapped	0·3	0·1	0·1	0·3	0·3

Source: Tsentralnoe Statisticheskoe Upravlenie. *Narodnoe khozyaystvo SSSR v 1969 g.* (Moscow 1970), 666.

Bearing in mind the limitations due to small size, the administration, organisation and pattern of work in the primary schools corresponds to that of the lower section of the eight-year schools which is given below.

The eight-year (incomplete secondary) schools (*Vosmiletnie shkoly*) **and the first eight grades in the ten-year (complete secondary) schools** (*Desyatiletnie shkoly*) The eight-year (incomplete secondary) general education school provides compulsory co-education for children from the age of seven to the age of fifteen.

The ten-year (complete secondary) general education labour polytechnic school provides co-education for children and adolescents aged seven to seventeen. An eleven-year period of instruction may be established for the schools where the instruction is conducted in a language other than Russian, with the authorisation of the USSR Council of Ministers. This is in operation in the Baltic republics.

This section deals with education in the eight-year school and in the first eight grades in the ten-year school; education in the ninth and tenth (eleventh) grades is described in the next section on upper secondary education.

According to the Statutes of the Secondary General Education School of 8 September 1970, the main tasks of the schools of this kind are:

1. to give pupils a general secondary education which corresponds to the current demands of social, scientific and technical progress, to acquaint pupils with a sound knowledge of the principles of science and to enable them to enlarge this knowledge on their own;

2. to mould the marxist-leninist world outlook in the young generation and to instil in pupils the feelings of Soviet patriotism, love for homeland, for its people and for the Communist Party of the Soviet Union as well as the readiness to defend the socialist fatherland;

3. to ensure an all-round harmonious development of the pupils, their aesthetic and physical education, the strengthening of their health and the proper organisation of their labour train-

ing, to prepare them for life, for the conscious choice of an occupation and for full involvement in work and public activities.

The general character of the work at school links education with the process of communist construction and guarantees the upbringing of the young in the spirit of communist morality. The educational laws explicitly rule out any kind of religious influence in instruction and education of children at school.

Instruction in school is free and all pupils are given the opportunity to receive instruction in their mother tongue. This principle is generally applied to all indigenous ethnic groups, but does not include the Jewish minority in the USSR.

Instruction and education in secondary general education schools is provided in accordance with syllabuses and curricula approved by the Ministry of Education of the USSR. The Ministries of Education of the Union republics, the autonomous republics and the territorial and regional departments of public education are authorised, in agreement with the Ministry of Education of the USSR, to make any necessary changes in syllabuses and curriculum in the light of local conditions, subject to observance of the specified number of hours laid down in the curriculum for each grade. These prescribed hours of compulsory instruction per week vary with the age of the children; according to the 1970 Statutes it is 24 hours for grades one to four, 30 hours for grades five to eight and up to 32 hours for grades nine to ten (eleven).

In the lower grades lessons are normally given by one teacher, teaching all subjects. The mother tongue occupies almost half the school hours at this stage and includes writing, reading, speech training, grammar and caligraphy. The syllabus specifies the teaching methods, the themes, the readings to be covered both in class and at home, the excerpts or poems to be learned by heart, and the subjects to be studied in the individual lessons.

Apart from the native language, teaching is given throughout the lower grades in arithmetic, drawing and music, physical education and working habits. In the second grade the pupils start nature study and in the fourth grade, history. At this stage stress is put upon the formation of personal habits and good behaviour: tidiness, orderliness, politeness, punctuality and respect for elders.

In the upper grades pupils are taught the fundamentals of the natural and social sciences, and are introduced to the early stages of polytechnic education and the principles of scientific materialism. The curriculum at this stage includes the full range of school subjects and consists of the native language and literature, physics, mathematics, chemistry, biology, history, geography, a foreign language, drawing and technical drawing, singing and music education, physical education and labour training. The natural sciences and mathematics occupy an important place. In the school year 1967/8 the pupils in grades five to eight inclusive spent 1,565 hours on the natural sciences and mathematics, and 1,585 hours on humanities.

In general, the subjects studied in grades five to eight constitute an essential and indispensable preparation for the more advanced study in grades nine and ten in a complete secondary school. The study of the different subjects progresses with increasing complexity, extends over wider fields and embraces such matters as the growth of national literature, ancient, medieval and modern history, physical and human geography of the USSR and the world, botany, zoology, anatomy and physiology of man, the building up of an extensive vocabulary and mastering the rules of grammar and phonetics of a foreign tongue, advanced arithmetic, algebra, geometry, inorganic and organic chemistry, the study of the structure of matter, of light and sound, the knowledge of projections, mechanical and engineering drawing, artistic and decorative design, talks on the fine arts, Soviet art and its ideological content, gymnastics, athletics, swimming and team games.

Subjects such as mathematics, physics, chemistry and biology are taught in close connection with their importance for modern industrial production and agriculture. In addition, in the urban areas practical experience in industry is provided on a limited scale.

Another feature of the new curricula is the introduction of optional subjects (see p 66) in the seventh and eighth grades, though the full range of possible options (Russian, mathematics, physics, chemistry, history, geography, a foreign language) is only gradually being made available. The most popular of the options are mathematics, physics and foreign languages.

The length of the lessons in the secondary school is forty-five minutes. The breaks between lessons normally last ten minutes with a half-hour break after the second or the third lesson.

Great stress is put upon the moral education of the younger adolescent. The system of values transmitted by the school is based upon the concept of communist morality and emphasises the moral qualities associated with the ideal type of 'the new communist man'. These, at this stage of individual development, include: love for the fatherland, and for one's home town or village; a feeling of friendship for the children of all nations; respect for labour, industriousness, truthfulness, honesty, modesty, politeness; respect for Soviet achievements, love for the Communist Party and interest in the activities of the Soviet government, the Communist Party, and the Pioneer and Komsomol organisations.

Homework assignments are made by the teachers according to the prescribed daily load: in the first grade, up to one hour; in the second, up to one and a half hours; in the third and fourth grades, up to two hours; in the fifth and sixth, up to two and a half hours; in the seventh, up to three hours; in the eighth and higher grades, up to four hours.

Evaluation of the pupils' progress is made on a five-point scale: five (excellent), four (good), three (satisfactory), two (poor), one (very poor). Compulsory final examinations take place at the end of the eighth grade. In addition, at the decision of the Union republic Ministries of Education, end-of-year examinations may take place in the fourth, fifth, sixth and seventh grades. Pupils who obtain marks of five in all subjects at the end of a school year and who have participated actively in the life of the school are awarded commendations. Pupils who obtain unsatisfactory marks at the end of a school year in no more than two subjects receive summer assignments and, if these are successfully fulfilled, the pupil in question may be permitted by the school's pedagogic council to move on into the next grade. Pupils who obtain unsatisfactory marks at the end of the school year in more than two subjects must repeat the grade. Pupils who have failed to obtain satisfactory marks in a grade for the third time may be dismissed from the school if they are over fifteen.

In addition, pupils' conduct is very much taken into account and is evaluated as exemplary, satisfactory or unsatisfactory in each year. Unsatisfactory marks for conduct can only be recorded after a decision by the school's pedagogical council to this effect is taken. In cases of persistent insubordination to teachers or flagrant violation of the rules of discipline, pupils may, as an extreme form of punishment, be expelled from school. It is assumed that the pupils are under an obligation to study diligently, to conduct themselves in an exemplary manner, to take an active part in school life and socially useful labour and to observe at all times the Rules for Pupils. These insist upon diligence, punctuality in attendance, unquestioned obedience to the teachers, full attention during lessons, modest and respectful behaviour towards parents and loyalty to the school.

The methods of teaching reflect the general acceptance of the science of pedagogy with its formal structure and its system of rules prescribing a general pattern for the conduct of a lesson and the most effective ways for teaching particular concepts, ideas and procedures. Each lesson follows, therefore, a clearly defined sequence and consists, in the true Herbartian tradition, of easily identifiable parts. First, the teacher examines the pupils' homework, the answers to the set questions being given by selected pupils who are often called to the blackboard and asked to explain step by step how a particular answer was arrived at. This is a very important thing, as marks, which are carefully recorded, are given by the teacher for each individual performance. Words of praise, encouragement, criticism or scorn accompany the evaluation of a pupil's progress. Over a longer period of time each pupil is tested many times in order to have his true attainment assessed in each subject. Checking homework helps at the same time to recall the material covered so far by the teacher. The next stage is a clear and orderly exposition of the new material, the general principles being stated first and then illustrated with the help of a number

of concrete examples or exercises. More questions follow to make
sure that the new material has been fully understood. The teacher
then repeats the essential aspects of the work just covered and
links it with the material studied to date. He, or she, finally sets
new homework to be done for the next lesson. This is usually a
written assignment but may, alternatively, involve learning a
poem by heart or careful study of a selected extract from the
textbook or an additional source. The pattern is rigorously
observed in all grades, the assumption being that one makes
progress through hard work, concentration, diligence and perse-
verance which must receive the proper reward, just as slacking
off, carelessness and laziness must be penalised.

The administration of a school is exercised by its director who
is responsible to the state for the education of the pupils as well
as for the school's organisation and finance. In particular, his
duties include the selection and guidance of staff, supervision of
the ideological and political aspects of education, assisting the
Young Pioneers and the Komsomol organisations at school,
directing the work of the parents' committee and presenting
reports on the work of the school to the educational authorities.
The deputy director of a school is responsible for the organisation
of the teaching and upbringing of the pupils, the implementation
of the official curricula and the quality of instruction.

An organiser of extra-curricular educational activities is appointed by the district or city education department in each
secondary general education school. He is responsible for the
organisation and management of the extra-curricular activities
and socially useful labour of the pupils and offers help and advice
to the class teachers, subject teachers and other persons parti-
cipating in this kind of work. A senior Young Pioneer leader is
also appointed by the district or city department of education,
with the approval of the district or city Komsomol Committee, to
conduct the work of the Pioneer organisation in each school.

In order to give proper consideration to the many problems
arising in connection with the instruction and education of the
pupils, pedagogical councils have now been established in all
schools with more than three teachers. They consist of the

director of the school, the deputy director, the organiser of the extra-curricular activities, teachers of all subjects, the senior Pioneer leader, the school doctor, the librarian and the chairman of the parents' committee. Additionally, the representatives of the institution or organisation sponsoring the school, the pupils' parents and other persons may be invited to join the council in an advisory capacity. The function of the pedagogical council is principally to unify the efforts of the teaching staff and all other personnel, to improve the standard of general and polytechnic education of pupils and to perfect teaching methods.

Parents' committees are in existence in all schools for the purpose of ensuring permanent and close ties between the school and the parents. Their main task is enlisting the active assistance of parents in school activities, in organising self-help among the pupils, in spreading the knowledge of the principles of education and upbringing of children among the parents and in carrying out improvements in the material facilities at school.

Individual schools maintain close links with industrial enterprises, state or collective farms or other institutions or organisations exercising patronage over the school. These agencies offer concrete assistance to the school in improving its facilities, organising industrial practice wherever possible, assisting with extra-curricular activities, the establishment of vacation camps and vocational guidance of pupils.[3]

Mention should be made of two varieties of school which have gained popularity in recent years.

Prolonged day schools (*shkoly s prodlennym dnem*) are ordinary eight-year schools offering all their pupils the opportunity of staying on in the school in the afternoon and early evening. The extra time is spent under supervision on homework, games and group activities of all kinds including Pioneer meetings. The children return home in the evening, usually after having had their supper at school, which is paid for by the parents. The prolonged day schools appeared in 1960 and have quickly grown in number in the course of the last decade.

The so-called language schools teach a foreign language (usually English, French, German or Spanish) in a more intensive

E

way, normally from the second grade onward. They also often teach some of the other subjects in that language in the upper grades. Schools of this kind are found in the larger cities. It must be remembered that the schools of this type are not considered to be special in any way and that they base their work on an ordinary school curriculum. However, there are many parents who are keen on sending their children to a language school. As the applications for admission often exceed the number of vacancies, some selection is necessary. This is based on the ability of a child to reproduce certain foreign words or sounds and may well reflect differences in the home background.

Table 8

Curriculum in a Secondary General Education School

Subject	*Periods per week in classes:*										
	I	*II*	*III*	*IV*	*V*	*VI*	*VII*	*VIII*	*IX*	*X*	*Total*
Russian language	12	10	10	6	6	3	3	2	2/0	–	53
Literature	–	–	–	2	2	2	2	3	4	3	18
Mathematics	6	6	6	6	6	6	6	6	5	5	58
History	–	–	–	2	2	2	2	3	4	3	18
Social study	–	–	–	–	–	–	–	–	–	2	2
Nature study	–	2	2	2	–	–	–	–	–	–	6
Geography	–	–	–	–	2	3	2	2	2	–	11
Biology	–	–	–	–	2	2	2	2	0/2	2	11
Physics	–	–	–	–	–	2	2	3	4	5	16
Astronomy	–	–	–	–	–	–	–	–	–	1	1
Chemistry	–	–	–	–	–	–	2	2	3	3	10
Technical drawing	–	–	–	–	–	1	1	1	–	–	3
Foreign language	–	–	–	–	4	3	3	2	2	2	16
Art	1	1	1	1	1	1	–	–	–	–	6
Music	1	1	1	1	1	1	1	–	–	–	7
Physical education	2	2	2	2	2	2	2	2	2	2	20
Labour training	2	2	2	2	2	2	2	2	2	2	20
Total	24	24	24	24	30	30	30	30	30	30	276
Options	–	–	–	–	–	–	2	4	6	6	18

Source: Ministry of Education of the USSR. *Public Education in the Soviet Union* (Moscow 1968), 102.

Schools for the physically and mentally handicapped
(*Shkoly spetsialnogo vospitaniya i obucheniya anomalnykh detey*)
A system of differentiated types of school providing special
education and care for children suffering from various kinds
of disability includes special schools for mentally handicapped
children, deaf children, blind children, children with weak hear-
ing, children with poor eyesight, children with speech defects and
with sensory motor disturbances.

Owing to the general improvement in the standard of health
and sanitation, an early detection of a particular disability is now
possible, so that special facilities can be provided by the time of
compulsory education. As a result more than 300,000 children
attended schools of the above-mentioned types in the school year
1967/8. Many of the special schools are boarding schools, each
providing education appropriate for the children suffering from
a given disability. Most of the day schools are situated in large
towns and often have special kindergartens attached to them. All
republics now have schools for mentally handicapped, deaf and
blind children.

The curricular patterns follow the work of the ordinary
schools. In addition, blind children are taught practical skills
such as making musical instruments, needlework, basketry or
the skills required in certain kinds of factories, so that after
completing their education they may get a job without additional
training.

Teachers for special schools are trained in special faculties and
departments in the pedagogic institutes in Moscow, Leningrad,
Kiev, Minsk, Sverdlovsk and Irkutsk.

National schools (*Natsionalnye shkoly*)   In the so-called
national schools the language of instruction is not Russian, but
the native language of the people. The national schools constitute
the majority of schools in the Union republics, other than the
RSFSR, and in the autonomous republics. In the RSFSR there
were 10,436 national schools in the school year 1965/6. Of these
5,506 were primary schools, 3,572 eight-year schools and 1,358
ten-year schools. Instruction was given in forty-two different
native languages, of which six were the languages of other Union

republics (Azerbaidzhani, Armenian, Georgian, Estonian, Kazakh and Turkmeni).[4]

In the autonomous republics and regions, instruction is often given in both the local language and the language of the republic; for instance in the RSFSR the eight-year schools in the Mordovian, Chuvash, Udmurt, Yakut, Bashkir and other autonomous republics use the local language as the language of instruction, while instruction in the upper secondary grades is in Russian. In Northern Caucasus and in the Far North the primary grades use local languages and the middle and upper secondary grades use Russian, although the native language is retained as one of the subjects of the curriculum. Russian language is taught in the national schools from the first or the second grade.[5]

The question whether the proportion of national schools in the different republics approximately corresponds to the proportion of non-Russian population in the area is not easy to answer. On the whole, the evidence seems to suggest that the percentage of children in the schools with Russian as a language of instruction exceeds the percentage of Russians in the different Union republics, but only by 2–13 per cent, except for Moldavia, Kirghizstan and Kazakhstan, where it is around 20 per cent.[6]

Boarding schools (*Shkoly internaty*)   The boarding schools came into prominence with the Khrushchev reforms in the late 1950s. Their stated aim was to provide for the needs of children who had lost their parents or whose home life was not satisfactory, but other considerations, such as experimenting with this type of school as an alternative to home upbringing, may also have played a part.

The boarding schools may be eight-year or ten-year schools and their curriculum is identical with that of the ordinary day school. The daily programme includes, however, activities of all kinds in the time not set aside for meals, homework, physical exercise and sleep.

Classrooms, laboratories and a gymnasium constitute the section of the school devoted to instructional purposes, while a refectory, a reading room, a library, a Pioneer room and the dormitories constitute the other section.

The staff is composed of teachers and tutors. The former, usually living outside, teach the various school subjects, while the latter live in the school and take care of the children outside the classrooms, after lessons.

Tuition in the boarding schools is free. The parents have to pay, however, for the children's upkeep, the parental contribution depending upon income and generally being between 10 and 70 per cent of the actual cost. Children from large families are exempt from any payment. The parents of other children may pay anything between 5 and 35 roubles per month. Pupils may be visited by their parents on any day and may go home for Saturday afternoon and Sunday, if the parents so desire.

Boarding schools should not be confused with children's homes (*detskie domy*), which take children of all ages who are without parents, bringing them up and sending them to a nearby school for regular instruction.

UPPER SECONDARY GENERAL, SPECIALISED AND VOCATIONAL EDUCATION

The system of differentiated post-compulsory education consists of the following main types of school:

1. secondary general education labour polytechnic schools (grades nine and ten), offering full-time education;

2. secondary specialised schools offering both full-time and part-time education;

3. vocational-technical schools, offering both full-time and part-time education;

4. Schools for Working and Rural Youth, offering general part-time education.

After the successful completion of the eight years of universal, compulsory education the pupils can, therefore, local circumstances permitting, study full-time in secondary general education, secondary specialised education or vocational-technical schools, or enter into full-time employment with the opportunity of continuing education on a part-time basis in Schools for Working and Rural Youth, secondary specialised or vocational-technical schools.

Secondary general education labour polytechnic schools (grades nine and ten)   Upper secondary general education is provided in grades nine and ten (in the Baltic republics grades nine to eleven) of the secondary general education labour polytechnic school. According to the 1959 Statute on the Secondary General Education Labour Polytechnic School the aim of this type of school is an all-round development of pupils' capacities, education in the spirit of communism and the production of young people with a good basic knowledge of science who are also capable of systematic physical work.

The purpose of the Khrushchev reform in 1958 was 'to bring schools closer to life' and to close the widening gulf between intellectual and manual work by introducing three years of upper secondary general education instead of two and using the additional time for production training. In fact, a third of the time in the three upper grades was to be spent on general technical subjects, production training and productive work.

However, the full-scale transition to a three-year course with two days each week devoted to practical work in agriculture or industry encountered great difficulties. First, the industrial enterprises and state farms found it difficult, considering their production targets and the pressure to improve labour efficiency, to accommodate large numbers of pupils on a permanent basis and provide facilities adequate and meaningful enough for them. Neither the managers of the individual enterprises nor the workers gained anything from the new measures. Secondly, the teachers began to express their growing doubts about the value of the pupils' work, which in reality often had to be confined to simple, repetitive and auxiliary activities. Thirdly, the pupils themselves and their parents showed little enthusiasm for the innovation which in practice offered much less than had originally been anticipated. The result was a return to the two-year course with a drastic reduction in the time devoted to industrial training and practical work in industry and agriculture.

The curriculum in grades nine and ten is based upon the knowledge acquired by pupils in the lower secondary grades. Emphasis is put upon the study of Russian language and literature, mathematics, history and physics. Included also are social science, geography, biology, astronomy, chemistry, a foreign tongue, physical education and labour training. The prescribed number of lessons per week is thirty for both grades. In addition, the official timetable prescribes six optional lessons (see p 66) per week for each grade.

The syllabus in literature covers the study of the great Russian writers of the nineteenth century, such as Turgenev, Chekhov, Goncharov, Chernyshevsky, Nekrasov and Tolstoy, and Soviet poets and writers such as Gorky, Mayakovsky, Sholokhov and Fadeyev. It includes also the great works of the Western poets such as Shakespeare and Goethe, the study of the literature of the peoples of the USSR as well as of the basic features of Soviet literature in its world significance, with a special stress upon its ideological preoccupations.

Mathematics includes algebra, geometry and trigonometry in grade nine, and an advanced study of the three subdivisions of the subject in grade ten.

History covers Russian history, Soviet history and world history. Considerable attention is paid to the rise and growth of 'scientific communism', to the October Revolution, the economic growth of the USSR, World War II and the political and economic changes in the world since then.

Geography, taught in grade nine only, covers an intensive study of the economic geography of the USSR, other aspects and areas having been covered in the previous years.

In physics, the pupils study mechanics, heat, molecular physics, electricity, optics and atomic structures. Astronomy is taken as a separate subject in grade ten, while chemistry, inorganic and organic, receives considerable attention in both grades.

The study of a foreign language (a school usually offers only one) concentrates upon the sound mastery of an extensive vocabulary and on grammar and syntax. Particular attention is now given to oral practice. Most common is the study of English, this being followed by French, German, Spanish and some of the Eastern languages.

Labour training attempts to acquaint the pupils with the most important branches of present-day industrial and agricultural production and to introduce them to work in these fields. The study of basic production problems is organised differently in urban and rural schools.

Mechanical and electrical engineering feature in the urban schools. Pupils of both sexes study machine parts and their assembly, principles of construction, and operation of the particular parts of different kinds of machine; they become familiar with the various kinds of raw materials and carry out practical work, generally in the school workshops.

In schools in rural areas the pupils are given a fundamental knowledge of agricultural production and cattle breeding, and they study the problems of mechanisation and electrification of agriculture. In addition they are organised into production brigades and perform work of different kinds on the state and collective farms.

Military training for boys only, which covers military drill, target practice shooting with rifles and submachine guns and the study of military regulations, is conducted during one of the two hours allocated to physical education. Recently, military advisers with appropriate qualifications have been appointed in secondary schools to organise and conduct the military training of pupils.

The option courses are of two kinds. Complementary courses supplement the body of knowledge included in the ordinary subjects and serve to deepen the contents of the standard syllabus. Special courses are concerned with specific themes or topics which can be handled quite separately from the ordinary syllabus. The full range of options includes mathematics, physics, chemistry, biology, geography, history, technical drawing, Soviet literature, foreign languages and art.

Teaching methods remain formal and put great demand upon both the teachers and pupils in terms of the content that has to be mastered and retained. The teacher is held personally responsible for fully covering the whole syllabus prescribed for each grade, for adequate elucidation of all points, and for making sure that both classwork and homework are executed by all pupils in the proper manner. The pupils are faced with very stiff demands and must work very hard to make the grade. Failure is generally ascribed to the lack of effort, laziness, lack of proper attention in the classroom and not to intellectual deficiency on the part of any pupil. As a rule no allowances are made for genuine difficulties that pupils may have in particular subjects, and the threat of having to repeat a grade hangs heavily upon some. There is a general assumption that learning requires application and a real effort and that it is a sacred duty for each pupil to work hard.

Extra-curricular activities also play an important role at this stage. There are regular meetings of hobby circles and clubs, both on the school premises and out of school. Special lectures, talks and reports on problems of interest for pupils in science, engineering and the arts are frequently arranged at school. Matinees and parties to mark historical events of all kinds are also held, with the co-operation of outstanding writers, scientists, artists or military men. Visits are made to exhibitions, museums, historic sites, theatres, cinemas, beauty spots and exhibitions of children's technical and artistic achievements. Tourism and the study of local folklore have very much expanded in recent years and many older pupils have taken part in long hikes and special expeditions to explore the geography and the historic past of the different regions. Physical training and participation in various sporting activities take place in a growing number of sports palaces, open arenas and parks. An enormous effort has been made to provide extended opportunities for pupils to spend their holidays in summer camps run by school and Komsomol. At the same time there is a determined effort to recruit as many pupils as possible for active participation in the work of the Komsomol, in order to intensify their political commitment and strengthen their loyalty to the state and the Communist Party.

Examinations are an important means of testing the pupils' knowledge. Of crucial importance is the final leaving examination, at the end of the tenth grade, for the award of the certificate of maturity (*attestat zrelosti*). This includes literature, mathematics, physics, chemistry, history, social science and a foreign language. The first examination is a written composition on Russian literature with a choice of one out of three subjects. The second written examination is in mathematics. Examinations in other subjects are oral, the pupils being examined by a committee of a number of teachers of the given subject or a related one, and headed by the director of the school or his deputy to assure objectivity. Every year the questions for the examination are published four to five months in advance. This procedure is adopted in order to indicate the material which should be systematised and revised in preparation for the examination and to avoid overburdening the pupils' memory with too much information.

The general supervision of the examinations rests with the Ministries of Education of the Union republics, which are responsible for the approval of the texts or topics for the written examinations and of the questions for the oral examinations in the form of examination cards, as well as for establishing the criteria for the evaluation and award of marks.

At the end of the tenth year every pupil gets three marks: the end-of-year mark, based upon continuous assessment of his progress throughout the year, the examination mark and the final mark. The last one is based upon the first two and reflects, therefore, both the results of day-to-day work and the pupil's ability to present the fruits of several years' work in one single performance. This is seen by the Soviet educationists not as a completely objective and entirely satisfactory method of assessment but as a sound one, considering the shortcomings of other alternatives.

The certificate of maturity entitles the holders to apply for admission to the universities and the establishments of higher education in general, but whether or not a candidate is admitted depends normally on the results of the entrance examination held by the particular institution.

Secondary specialised schools (*Srednie spetsialnye uchebnye zavedeniya*) Secondary specialised schools offer courses of study on full-time day and part-time evening and correspondence basis. They accept young men and women aged fifteen to thirty with an eight-year general education. In most secondary specialised schools admission is by a competitive entrance examination and the courses of study vary in length from three to four and a half years. Alternatively, pupils with complete secondary general education may be accepted for shortened courses of study, varying in length from one to three and a half years.

The secondary specialised schools' function is to produce technicians whose tasks in the process of production are:

1. to act as the principal organisers and technical leaders in the primary stages of production;

2. to provide immediate servicing of automated and other types of machinery;

3. to act as assistant engineers.

The present system of secondary specialised education in the USSR includes technicums and other secondary educational establishments with different kinds of specialisation: industrial, economic, agricultural, technological, medical, pedagogical, as well as establishments specialising in transport, construction, communication and other fields.

Technicums (the name usually refers to larger establishments teaching a wider range of subdivisions of a particular specialisation) train electricians, mechanics, production planners, statisticians, commodity specialists as well as agricultural and stockbreeding technicians. The full-time courses include four subdivisions:

1. senior courses in certain specialisations in industry, transport, construction and communications, including one to one and a half years' work period during which the students take correspondence or evening courses;

2. courses in public health, physical culture, pedagogy, economics and art which are accompanied by obligatory training in the field;

3. courses to train specialists in agriculture, geology and seasonal work of certain kinds which combine theoretical and practical lessons with work on model farms, state and collective farms and in certain types of industrial enterprises;

4. courses with alternating periods of theoretical studies and productive work throughout the whole length of the course of study.

Part-time evening or correspondence study can be undertaken either in the evening courses and correspondence departments of the full-time establishments or in independent correspondence or evening technicums. In 1964 there were 260 independent evening technicums and 50 independent correspondence technicums in addition to 1,125 evening departments and 1,877 correspondence study departments in large full-time institutions.

In the school year 1969/70, of the 4,301,700 students in secondary specialised establishments, 1,898,800 studied in establishments specialising in industry and construction, 367,900 in transport and communications, 667,700 in agriculture, 456,000 in economics and law, 438,500 in health, physical culture and sport, 366,500 in education and 106,300 in the arts.[7] It is interesting to observe that in the course of the last decade there has been an increase in the proportion of full-time students (from 53 per cent in 1960/1 to 56 per cent in 1969/70), a decline in the proportion of the evening students (from 18 per cent in 1960/1 to 16 per cent in 1969/70) and a slight decline in the proportion of students studying by correspondence (from 29 per cent in 1960/1 to 28 per cent in 1969/70).

Competition for entry is often very keen in the case of well-known technicums, such as the radio-technicum in Leningrad, established in 1930 and nowadays educating over 5,000 young men and women in radio engineering and radio electronics.

The students in the secondary specialised education establishments are given both general education, approximating to that in an upper general secondary education school as well as specialised education of technical character in the field of their choice. In addition, they receive broad polytechnic training and do practical work in machine workshops. Specialised training is, therefore, linked to and based upon general and polytechnic education. During their course of study the students have to take regular tests and examinations. Correspondence students submit written reports which are marked by the teachers or are examined orally. Students' progress is assessed on the usual marking scale of five to one.

Full-time students in secondary specialised education establishments are awarded government scholarships and those who have to live away from their usual place of residence are also provided with lodgings in students' hostels. Special concessions are offered to the students studying without interrupting their work. Over and above the regular annual holidays, students in the first and second years studying in the evening are given ten extra days and those studying by correspondence, thirty days of paid leave. The students in the third and fourth years get twenty days if they study in the evening and forty days if they study by correspondence. When they prepare for the final examination, the evening and correspondence students get an additional thirty days' paid leave; and if they have to write and defend a diploma paper, two months' paid leave. Students in their final year can also take an additional month's leave without pay for practical training in the field of their specialisation or to prepare the diploma paper. Finally, in their last year students may be given one day off per week on half-pay and, if necessary, one or two days more without pay. The generous nature of these provisions has, however, increased the real cost of part-time education in terms of the time off productive work.

On leaving, the students obtain both a professional qualification and a certificate of secondary education which makes them eligible for admission to higher education establishments. In reality, the majority go straight into full-time employment.

Each school has a director, appointed by a ministry, government department, council of national economy or the executive committee of the council of workers' deputies under whose jurisdiction it comes. He is selected from a list of specialists with the necessary industrial and pedagogical qualifications. The director exercises an overall control of the school. He is responsible for the appointments to the staff, the admission of students, the organisation and fulfilment of curricular plans, the material and financial aspects of work. A deputy director of studies is appointed on the nomination of the director and is responsible for the quality of educational and methodological work, for industrial training and for improving the quality of instruction.

The school's pedagogical council examines all problems of

teaching methods, production training and student welfare. The members of the council are the director, his deputy, the heads of the methodological committee, teachers in charge of departments or branches, superintendents of workshops, instructors in charge of production training, the librarian and the representatives of social organisations in the school.

Each secondary specialised education establishment is attached to an enterprise, organisation or institution whose work closely corresponds to the skills being studied by its students. Many possess branches in other towns or areas in order to offer opportunities for study to wider sectors of the working population. Due to progressing industrialisation and mechanisation in the USSR, this type of school is bound to go on expanding and providing the national economy with properly qualified skilled labour.

Vocational-technical schools (*Professionalno-tekhnicheskie uchilishcha*)   Vocational-technical schools constitute another important sector of education. Their main task is to train, on a planned basis, skilled workers and junior technical personnel for all branches of the national economy. The significance of schools of this kind is constantly growing because of the rapid development of production techniques and modern technology.

The system of vocational-technical education was instituted in the 1930s and reorganised in 1940 under the State Labour Reserves. It is now under the State Committee of the USSR Council of Ministers for Vocational-Technical Education. Its importance and expansion in the period 1951–70 can be seen from Table 9. The numbers of students who finished courses of training of this type were 493,000 in 1950, 741,000 in 1960, 1,100,000 in 1965 and just over 1,500,000 in 1969.[8]

Since 1959 vocational-technical schools have been organised into urban and rural establishments. The urban schools train workers for different branches of industry, construction, transport and communications. The rural schools train workers for agriculture.

Vocational-technical schools offer both full-time courses and part-time evening courses. Admission is open to students with eight years of compulsory education behind them. As a result the

Table 9
Number of Vocational-Technical Schools and Students (1951–70)

	Number of schools	Number of students (in 000)
1951	2,593	520
1961	3,684	1,064
1966	4,319	1,599
1967	4,791	1,886
1968	4,940	2,047
1969	5,064	2,113
1970	5,197	2,252

Source: Tsentralnoe Statisticheskoe Upravlenie. *Narodnoe khozyaystvo SSSR v 1969 g.* (Moscow 1970), 550.

minimum age for admission is fifteen, while the upper age limit varies from school to school, depending upon specialisation, and may be as low as seventeen or as high as twenty-five.

The courses vary in length from six months to three years but over the last ten years there has been a tendency to reduce the length of training because of the extension of compulsory education from seven to eight years in 1958 and the consequent improvement in the standard of general education among the new entrants.

As a result, in the early 1960s the length of training in eighty-six trades was cut from three to two and a half years. This applied, for example, to the training of setters and adjusters of various kinds of machines and equipment, instrument mechanics, electric fitters for servicing automatic machines and devices, assistant locomotive drivers, builders in a number of combined trades and chemical equipment operators. In eighty trades the length of training was shortened from two to one and a half years. Included in this group were foundry moulders, sharpeners, tooth cutters, grinders, mechanical assembly fitters, markers, workers engaged in hot metal treatment, electric locomotive drivers, radio and TV mechanics, reinforcement and concrete placers, rail-carriage repair fitters and workers in certain branches of the textile industry. Training was reduced from two years to one in sixty-six trades, including quality controllers of various goods, certain workers in the metallurgical industry, bricklayers, house painters, finishers, structure erectors and film projectionists. For tool-makers, equipment repair fitters, computer mechanics, excavator operators and press-mould engravers training was cut by one year, from three to two years.

In 1966 the Central Committee of the CPSU and the Council of Ministers of the USSR adopted a resolution, On Expanding Vocational Training and Providing Employment in the National Economy for the General Education School Leavers, which opened the way for shortened courses of vocational-technical training to the pupils who have finished the tenth grade of secondary general education school. The total number of specialisations taught at this level increased to over 1,000 in the school year 1969/70.

The education of students in vocational-technical schools is based upon uniform and compulsory curricula and programmes for each particular specialisation. In general, these consist of production studies occupying 60 per cent or more of the total number of hours of instruction; specialist technical subjects such as specialist technology, knowledge of materials, general technology of metals, mechanisation and automation, economics and organisation of production and technical drawing, amounting to 20 per cent; and general education subjects such as physics, mathematics, Russian or the mother tongue, elementary mechanics and industrial technology, social science, political, aesthetic and physical education, covering the remaining 20 per cent. The system combines, therefore, both theoretical and practical aspects of education.

Production training involves the study of production in workshops and teaching sections as well as training in industrial enterprises. The students learn to use the various kinds of industrial equipment in the factories, study the latest methods of production and principles of organisation of production. The process of training in the enterprises begins with group training in small training sections, continues with group training in production sections and the fulfilment of production tasks by the students working within groups of skilled workers, and finishes with the training of individual students in an independent use of the different kinds of machine and industrial equipment.

Students' progress is checked by a system of controls. These are instituted at three levels: concurrent, periodical and final. Current control takes place each time a student learns a new skill or masters a new technique. Periodical control occurs at the end of each semester and takes the form of test-work which helps to verify the knowledge, skills and experience acquired during that time. The final control is at the end of the year and at the end of the training period, and takes the form of a final examination and trial work. The final examination includes also oral and written tests and decides the grade and, therefore, the remuneration of the student when he takes up employment at the completion of his training.

Judging from recent pronouncements on the subject an attempt is to be made in the forthcoming years to improve the quality of education and the level of instruction in the vocational-technical schools, so that parity of status can eventually be established between them and the technicums, paving the way to universal and equivalent upper secondary education for all. This is a very ambitious plan, however, which can only be achieved over a longer period of time.

Extra-curricular activities in vocational-technical schools are extensive. The majority of students attend one kind of technical hobby circle or another. Music, dancing, singing and dramatic circles are also popular. So are physical culture and sports of all kinds.

Each vocational-technical school has its patron. This usually is a large industrial enterprise. It helps the school by providing it with new equipment, tools and machines, as well as by offering production training facilities for the students. The school, in return, often makes parts of equipment or components for the patron enterprise and regularly supplies it with a stream of qualified workers.

The students in vocational-technical schools receive state scholarships, are provided with overalls and are paid for their work during production training.

F

Schools for the gifted   The schools for gifted children include, broadly speaking, those for the artistically gifted and those for children exceptionally gifted in subjects like mathematics and the natural sciences.

Schools for children who display special aptitudes for music or dance from an early age have a long tradition behind them. There are at present many schools of this kind in the country. The best known are the Central Music School in Moscow and the ballet schools in Moscow, Leningrad and Kiev. Children are accepted at the age of seven, having been carefully chosen on the basis of individual tests for outstanding talent. The normal curriculum in general subjects is followed, combined with an intensive training in singing, playing a musical instrument, or in ballet dancing. If, after a certain period of time it is clear that the child's aptitudes do not justify the hopes placed in them, the child may be transferred to an ordinary school and continue practising his skills in hobby circles or out of school. Those who complete the course provided by the music schools move on to the music conservatories. Ballet school pupils study up to the age of nineteen and graduate from the schools with the diploma of Ballet Artist (*Artist Baleta*).

The schools for gifted mathematicians or natural scientists had their origin in the proposals of Professor Keldysh, the President of the Academy of Sciences of the USSR, and of the President of the Novosibirsk branch of the Academy, Professor Lavrentiev. The two scientists urged, in the interests of scientific and technological progress, that boys and girls with a special talent for mathematics should receive special attention and be given opportunities for intensive study of the subject and the related fields early in their lives, long before reaching the university.

When the idea became acceptable, in the middle 1960s, mathematical olympiads were organised to select the best pupils. The leading part was played by the University of Novosibirsk. Since that time, regular olympiads have been organised every year, first at the district, then at the provincial and finally at all-Siberian level. In August every year some 800 selected candidates are brought to Novosibirsk for four weeks in a vacation camp. A final choice of the best 400 is made on the basis of tests and competitions, and these are then admitted to the school organised at the University.

The school consists of grades eight, nine and ten, the students being normally admitted to grade eight. The curriculum covers all subjects, but more time is devoted to mathematics, physics and chemistry than in an ordinary school. Lessons are given in these subjects by professors of the Novosibirsk University and the Academy of Sciences. Supervised work is carried out in groups of ten to fifteen students, with the emphasis on individual research and the finding of solutions to specially set theoretical problems. In this the methods of study approximate to university work as the school tries to develop scientific thinking and mathematical logic. Intellectual games are employed and, in their last year, the students begin to participate in the scientific work of the Academy, whose laboratories are open to them.

Although some 10 per cent of the students do not finish the school, the rest complete the course and take the leaving examination, in the same way as other secondary school pupils. The students then take an entrance examination to the University of Novosibirsk together with other candidates. The rate of success is high. In 1964, out of 93 students of the school, 85 were admitted; in 1965, out of 110 students, 80 were accepted. This compares very favourably with the results obtained by the candidates for admission from the regular secondary schools.[9]

Similar schools in mathematics, physics and chemistry have now also been organised by the University of Moscow, and also in other centres. The introduction of schools of this type is an interesting development. One of the principles of the Soviet system has always been to educate children in the same type of school up to the age of fifteen and to provide for academic, technical and vocational differentiation only after this age has been attained. The creation of schools for a very small proportion of highly talented children at the age of fourteen, with the object of preparing young scientists of high calibre, is difficult to reconcile with that principle. None the less, selection at fourteen, based upon a relatively uniform basis of similar kinds of opportunities for all children before the attainment of that age, is not the same thing as irrevocable selection and differentiation through entirely different types of school at an early age. The appearance of this kind of school in the USSR makes it clear, however, that political and scientific imperatives do not always coincide with each other.

Military schools (*Voyennye uchilishcha*)   Military boarding schools named after General Suvorov prepare cadets for service in the Soviet armed forces. Established in 1943, they originally admitted the sons of soldiers who had been killed in the war. Now the sons of the army and navy personnel are given preference. The schools admit boys who have finished the primary grades and offer complete secondary education leading to the award of certificate of maturity with the possibility of subsequent advanced military training in a military academy.

YOUTH ORGANISATIONS

The youth organisations in the USSR are very closely associated with the extra-curricular activities in schools and their work is integrated with the general education of the young. They consist of the Octobrists, for children up to the age of ten; the Pioneers, for those aged ten to fifteen; and the Komsomol, for young people of fifteen to twenty-eight.

The Octobrists   Children in primary grades may join the Octobrists, attached to the Pioneer groups operating in the schools. The first Octobrists appeared in 1924, were temporarily discontinued and re-established in November 1957 by decision of the Eighth Plenum of the Central Committee of the Komsomol.

The function of the Octobrists is primarily to instil into young children a firm desire to join the Pioneers. At the same time certain general rules of behaviour are stressed: Octobrists love their schools, respect the old, and work hard: *tolko tekh kto lyubit trud oktyabryatami zovut* ('only those who love labour can be called Octobrists').

The Octobrists wear little red stars bearing a miniature portrait of Lenin on their school uniform. When out on a country walk or an excursion the group carries a small red flag. In charge of groups are members of the Komsomol or older Pioneers.

The Pioneers   The All-Union Lenin Pioneer Organisation
(*Vsesoyuznaya Pionerskaya Organizatsiya Imeni Lenina*) operates
under the general guidance of the CPSU.

The Pioneers came into being in Moscow in May 1922. In 1924
there were 170,000 members and the numbers grew quickly to
reach 13 million in 1949, around 15 million in 1960 and about
24 million in 1970. Today, despite its voluntary character, practically all children of the age group ten to fifteen belong to the
organisation, a clear indication of the paramount importance of
the Pioneers for Soviet society.

The explicit aim of the Pioneers is

> . . . to bring up children in the spirit of love and devotion to the
> Motherland, friendship between nations and proletarian inter-
> nationalism; to develop in them a conscientious attitude towards
> learning, love of work and curiosity; to bring up children as
> all-round developed individuals, conscientious, healthy, coura-
> geous, full of joy of life and unafraid of difficulties and as future
> builders of communism.[10]

The organisation consists of units based upon schools or, less
frequently, the children's homes. The basic unit for each class is
an *otryad* (detachment), and for the whole school a *druzhina*
(brigade). If there are enough members in an *otryad*, it can be
further subdivided into *zvena* (links). In 1970 there were 118,000
brigades and 800,000 detachments of the Pioneers in the USSR.
The work of each brigade is planned and organised by a brigade
council, the members of the council and its chairman being
elected by the Pioneers of the whole school. Their work is guided
by the Senior Pioneer Leader, who is an adult member of the
Komsomol and a full-time member of the school staff (sometimes
also a teacher). Each detachment has its council and chairman,
elected by the detachment. The leaders of the detachments are
younger members of the Komsomol.

Admission to the Pioneer organisation takes place in a special
ceremony. The candidates, having been approved by the brigade
council, attend the ceremony, during which they recite the
solemn Pioneer promise, receive red scarves and badges with the

inscription *vsegda gotov* (always ready), and acknowledge the red flag. The Pioneer promise runs as follows:

> I, a Young Pioneer of the Soviet Union, in the presence of my comrades solemnly promise to love my Soviet Motherland with all my heart and to live, learn and struggle as the great Lenin bade us and the Communist Party teaches us.[11]

The activities of the Pioneers include work in hobby clubs and circles, sport, games, competitions of various kinds, participation in festivals, exhibitions and displays, attending Pioneer holiday camps in the summer, making trips and excursions, producing their own plays and concerts. The Pioneers may also take part in socially useful work, such as helping the old and the infirm, performing tasks for the benefit of the school, the city or the local community.

Pioneer activities can take place in the schools or in Pioneer palaces or houses, young technicians' and young naturalists' stations, excursion and tourist stations. The number of these have been increasing quickly in recent years. In 1960 there were 3,148 palaces and houses of Pioneers and schoolchildren, 348 young technicians' stations and 272 young naturalists' stations. In 1969 the numbers rose to 3,781 palaces and houses of Pioneers and schoolchildren, 553 young technicians' stations and 327 young naturalists' stations. In that year there were also 168 excursion and tourist stations, 171 children's parks and 33 children's railways, where young railway enthusiasts can be introduced to the different kinds of work on a railway.[12]

Pioneer palaces represent the best and the largest complexes of general facilities for all kinds of extra-curricular activities. In Moscow the palace is a modern structure, situated in the Lenin Hills area. In Leningrad, Riga and Odessa the palaces are former aristocrats' residences. The Moscow palace, opened in 1962, possesses an attractive entrance hall with a small pool and a botanical garden, two large halls dedicated to Lenin and children's friendship, two theatres, where plays are staged and films are shown; numerous study rooms with facilities for the pursuit of subjects such as literature, nature study, music, geography and art; workshops for radio construction, making models, developing and printing films; a space-travel room and a games room for the younger children; gymnasia, ballet and dancing rooms, as well as a sports stadium with room for 7,000 spectators. The 60 circles and 800 activity groups provide opportunities for regular meetings for several thousands of Moscow children, generally in the ten to fifteen age group. Each group meets twice a week for two hours, under an instructor or a teacher, of whom there are over 500.

Pioneer houses conduct similar activities on a much more limited, local scale.

The Komsomol   The All-Union Lenin Communist League of Youth (*Vsesoyuznyi Leninskii Kommunisticheskii Soyuz Molodyozhi*) is a mass political organisation for young men and women aged fifteen to twenty-eight.

The Komsomol came into being in October 1918. In 1924 it was named after Lenin. Its original membership of 22,000 in 1918 increased to 1 million in 1925, 10 million in 1941, 23 million in 1966 and 28 million in 1970. In other words almost half of the age group now belong to the Komsomol; some ten years ago the proportion was about a third.

Leonid Brezhnev, in his Report of the Central Committee of the CPSU to the Twenty-fourth Party Congress in 1971, stressed again the aims of the organisation in the following words:

> The Komsomol's central task has been and remains to bring up young people in the spirit of communist ideas and devotion to our Soviet Motherland, in the spirit of internationalism, and actively to propagate the norms and cultural values of our society.[13]

The Report stressed the fact that in recent years the Komsomol has become more active socially and politically. The links between the CPSU and the Komsomol have been intensified: in the course of the five years 1966–71 almost half of the new members who joined the Party were from the ranks of the Komsomol; in the same period the number of CPSU members working in the Komsomol has doubled. It was almost impossible to name a sector of economic or cultural development where the energy, creative initiative and ardour of Komsomol members had not been displayed.

In a speech concerning the tasks of the Komsomol, delivered during the Sixteenth Komsomol Congress in 1970, the secretary of the Central Committee of the Komsomol, E. Tyazhelnikov, put particular emphasis on the struggle for an increase in productivity of labour which he described as a matter of direct concern for every member of the organisation. He also called for a greater effort to raise the educational standards of the members, a drive to recruit more students in higher education as well as an all-out effort to help with the military training of youth.[14]

In organisation the Komsomol is modelled on the Communist Party structure. The basic units are the branches, under branch secretaries; these exist in all schools where there are older youths, in universities, farms, factories, offices and units of the armed forces. Of particular significance are branches at the universities, each faculty having its own branch. Higher units are district, regional and republican Komsomol committees. The highest central organ is the Komsomol Congress which elects the Central Committee to direct the work of the organisation between the Congresses.

New members are admitted through sponsors who can be Party or Komsomol members or the councils of the Pioneer brigades. Belonging to the Komsomol involves a member in numerous activities such as the regular meetings of the branch, socially useful work, work on the land at harvest time, preparations of festivals, demonstrations, sport activities and propaganda work among the people in general.

Notes to chapter 3 are on p 127

4
Higher and Adult Education

HIGHER EDUCATION

THE great importance of higher education lies in the fact that it prepares highly qualified personnel for all sectors of national life: cultural, economic, social, scientific and political. The character and quality of progress in all these fields, in any country, depends very much upon the character, quality and extent of higher education.

The importance which the Soviet government attaches to this sector of public education is best seen in the light of the officially declared aims of higher education. According to the Statute on the Higher Education Establishments of the USSR of 1961, the aims of education at this level are political, economic and scientific and, in more precise terms, require all the institutions in higher education to do the following:

1. To train highly qualified specialists educated in the spirit of marxism-leninism, well versed in both the latest achievements of science and technology at home and abroad, and in the practical aspects of production, capable of utilising modern technology to the utmost and of creating the technology of the future.
2. To carry out research that will contribute to the solution of the problems of building communism.
3. To produce textbooks and study aids of a high standard.
4. To train teachers and research workers.
5. To provide advanced training for specialists with higher education working in the various fields.
6. To disseminate scientific and political knowledge among the people.
7. To study the problems connected with the utilisation of graduates and with improving the quality of their training.[1]

The number of higher education establishments including universities, polytechnics, technological institutes, medical institutes, conservatories of music, institutes of fine arts, pedagogical institutes and other specialised establishments in the academic year 1969/70 was exactly 800. Five years earlier, in the academic year 1964/5, the number of higher education establishments was 754 and included 42 universities, 185 establishments in the field of industry and construction, 37 in transport and communications, 98 in agriculture, 40 in economics and law, 82 in public health, 16 in physical culture and sport, 208 in education and 46 in arts and cinematography.

The total number of students studying in the higher education establishments in the academic year 1969/70 was 4,549,600, nearly 80,000 more than in 1968/9. In the academic year 1950/1 there were 1,247,400 students and in 1960/1, 2,396,100 students. The rate of growth is, therefore, very high, the number of students almost doubling itself every decade, since 1950/1.[2]

Higher education studies include full-time day study, evening courses and correspondence courses. Generally, one institution combines all three forms of study, but there exist a number of institutes specialising exclusively in evening or correspondence courses. The qualifications obtained in any of the three forms of study are formally of equal status.

Of the almost 4,550,000 students in higher education in 1969/70, 47·0 per cent were taking full-time day courses, 14·7 per cent evening courses and 38·3 per cent were in correspondence courses. In the academic year 1960/1 the figures were 48, 10 and 42 per cent, respectively. The geographical distribution of higher education establishments and of the student body as well as the geographical differences in the higher education opportunities as measured by the number of students per 10,000 of population can be seen from Table 10.

Almost all the higher education establishments are state institutions and are maintained out of the state budget. The only exceptions are the establishments belonging to co-operative and special bodies (the Co-operative Institute, Higher Trade Union School, Patrice Lumumba University, etc).

Table 10

Numbers of Higher Education Establishments, Number of Students and
Numbers of Students per 10,000 Inhabitants in the Union Republics in
the Academic Year 1969/70

	Number of higher education establishments	Number of students (in 000)	Number of students per 10,000 of population
USSR	800	4,549·6	188
RSFSR	454	2,655·8	204
Ukraine	138	804·1	171
Byelorussia	28	137·3	153
Uzbekistan	38	231·9	194
Kazakhstan	43	195·7	152
Georgia	18	90·1	192
Azerbaidzhan	12	99·2	194
Lithuania	12	55·7	178
Moldavia	8	45·5	127
Latvia	10	40·4	171
Tadzhikstan	7	42·6	147
Kirghizstan	9	46·2	158
Armenia	12	53·4	214
Turkmenistan	5	29·2	135
Estonia	6	22·5	166

Source: Tsentralnoe Statisticheskoe Upravlenie. *Narodnoe khozyaystvo SSSR v 1969 g.* (Moscow 1970), 679, 681.

Administratively and financially higher education establishments may be subordinated to the Ministry of Higher and Secondary Specialised Education of the USSR or of a Union republic, or in case of several specialised establishments, to the corresponding ministries or departments.

Higher education is free and about three-quarters of the students receive state scholarships. An increasing number of students, however, receive scholarships directly from industrial enterprises and state or collective farms which send talented and promising young men and women to study in the establishments of higher education. These scholarships vary in amount, depending upon the year of study and the progress made by a student. In the mid 1960s the basic monthly rate of award for a student in the first, second, third and fourth year was 28 roubles, for a

student in the final, fifth or sixth year 33 roubles. Increase
for certain types of studies (technical, agronomic, legal, foreign
trade, interpreting, physical education, Far North, etc) was 7
roubles. In addition, for excellent progress a 25 per cent bonus
was paid. Students sent by enterprises received the state rates
plus 15 per cent.[3]

Students have free access to the use of books, journals, and
textbooks in the libraries, the use of laboratories and laboratory
materials, the use of sport facilities and equipment, medical
service and hospital treatment. A nominal payment is charged
for accommodation in a students' hostel.

Table 11
Numbers of Students in Higher Education Establishments
According to Nationality (in 000)

	1962/63	1969/70
Russians	1,803·8	2,716·3
Ukrainians	426·9	620·4
Byelorussians	85·0	129·2
Jews	79·3	110·1
Uzbeks	70·1	147·5
Kazakhs	51·8	98·2
Georgians	58·5	87·6
Tartars	51·1	83·7
Azerbaidzhanis	36·6	85·7
Lithuanians	31·8	48·9
Moldavians	15·9	30·7
Latvians	19·8	22·2
Kirghiz	11·9	24·4
Tadzhiks	13·5	27·3
Armenians	44·6	80·0
Turkmen	11·8	22·7
Estonians	15·4	18·4
Chuvash	11·5	15·7

Source: Tsentralnoe Statisticheskoe Upravlenie. *Narodnoe khozyaystvo SSSR
v 1969 g.* (Moscow 1970), 690.

Universities   There were forty-nine universities in the
Soviet Union at the beginning of 1970. They included the old and
famous universities established in the more distant past (Moscow
—1755, Tartu—1802, Vilnius—1803, Kazan—1804, Kharkov—

1805, St Petersburg, now Leningrad—1819, Kiev—1834, Odessa—1865, Tomsk—1880); the universities created shortly after 1917 (Voronezh—1918, Gorky—1918, Tbilisi—1918, Dnepropetrovsk —1918, Irkutsk—1918, Riga—1919, Baku—1919, Sverdlovsk—1920, Tashkent—1920, Erevan—1920, Minsk—1921, Vladivostok—1923); the universities established after World War II (Uzhgorod—1945, Kishinev—1946, Dushanbe—1948, Ashkhabad—1950, Frunze—1951) as well as the universities which came into being in more recent years (Novosibirsk, Kuibyshev, Yaroslavl, Krasnoyarsk, Krasnodar, Gomel and Ordzhonikidze).

Each university is divided into faculties which represent the major fields of study: physics, biology, philology, history, geography and so on. Each faculty possesses a number of departments; the faculty of philosophy, for example, usually has departments of marxism-leninism, scientific communism, the history of philosophy, logic and ethics and aesthetics, while the faculty of history may consist of the departments of the history of the USSR, the history of the Communist Party of the Soviet Union, modern and contemporary history, medieval history, ancient history, history of art, archaeology, ethnography and anthropology and the history of Soviet society.

The demand for university places is very strong and is growing stronger, due to the fact that more and more students complete full secondary education and obtain a certificate of maturity, which entitles them to apply for admission. The pressures of demand vary, however, from faculty to faculty and from university to university. Naturally, they are greatest in the case of the universities of Moscow and Leningrad, where in certain faculties ten students may apply for one place. Competition is, however, also keen in the universities in the capitals of the Union republics and in several of the new universities. Applicants must pass an entrance examination for the faculty of their choice and this includes papers in Russian language and literature. A candidate who fails to get in one year may try again.

A student in a university has between 4,500 and 5,500 hours of instruction in twenty to thirty-five subjects during his period of study. The latter depends upon the field of study and the nature of specialisation and varies generally between four and a half and five and a half years for full-time students. The work load decreases with the year of study. First year's students usually have 36 hours of lectures, seminar and laboratory work per week. This decreases to 32 hours in the second year, 30 hours in the third year, 24 in the fourth year and an even smaller number of hours in the fifth year, which is devoted to the preparation of the diploma project by each student.

The curricula consist of courses in political education, common and compulsory to all, a whole range of courses in the field of study of a student, physical and military training and a course in a foreign language. Two typical university curricula are given in Table 12 (opposite) and Table 13 (on p 99).

The courses in political education include the history of the CPSU, political economy, dialectical and historical materialism and history of philosophy. In political economy the syllabus covers two sections. The first is concerned with the features of the capitalistic system of production, the classical theories of wages, interest, capital and rent, the trade cycle, the theory of price formation and monopolies and the relationship between capitalism, imperialism and colonialism. The second section deals with the economic aspects of socialism, the development of a socialist economy, the character of the production process under socialism, economic aspects of the transition from socialism to communism and the laws of development of the world system of socialism.

The study of scientific communism is considered an integral part of marxism-leninism which should increase the political commitment of the students and make them active participants in the struggle for the victory of communism. It involves a detailed review of the political and socio-economic conflicts in the past and at the present, and an exposition of the policy, strategy and tactics of the CPSU.

The syllabus in the history of philosophy consists also of two parts. The first deals with the development of philosophical ideas since antiquity and examines the views of the ancient Greek, Roman and Chinese philosophers, Erasmus, Leonardo da Vinci,

Table 12

Russian Language and Literature

| No/Subject | Number of hours | | |
	Total	Lectures	Seminars and practical studies
1 *2*	*3*	*4*	*5*
1. History of the CPSU	220	120	100
2. Political economy	140	100	40
3. Dialectical and historical materialism	140	80	60
4. History of philosophy	70	70	–
5. Pedagogics	64	64	–
6. Logic	70	44	26
7. Psychology	54	36	18
8. Methodology of teaching the Russian language and literature	70	36	34
9. Foreign language	270	–	270
10. Latin	204	–	204
11. Fundamentals of linguistics	156	122	34
12. Modern Russian language	344	188	156
13. Russian dialectology	54	30	24
14. History of the Russian language	208	140	68
15. Old Slavonic language	84	54	30
16. Russian folklore	70	50	20
17. History of Russian literature	376	376	–
18. History of the literature of the USSR peoples	90	90	–
19. Ukrainian (or Byelorussian language)	68	–	68
20. Southern or Western Slavonic language	68	–	68
21. Foreign literature (including antiquity)	270	270	–
22. Fundamentals of literary studies	204	186	18
23. Pedagogical practice	6 weeks		
24. Production training	12 weeks		
25. Optional courses	400	256	144

Source: Prokofiev, M. A., and others. *Higher Education in the USSR* (Paris 1961), 48.

Copernicus, Galileo, Kepler, Campanella, More, Bacon, Spinoza, Leibniz, Newton, Descartes, Hobbes, Locke, Berkeley, Hume, Helvétius, Diderot, Holbach, Kant, Fichte, Hegel, Feuerbach, as well as of the Russian thinkers: Lomonosov, Radishchev, the Decabrists, Khomyakov, Kireyevsky, Aksakov, Samarin, Chaadayev, Granovsky, Belinsky, Herzen, Ogarev, Speshnev, Chernyshevsky, Dobrolyubov, Pisarev, Shelgunov, Dostoyevsky, Tolstoy, Lavrov, Tkachev, Bakunin, Mikhailovsky, Katkov, Chicherin, Kavelin, Solovev and others. The second part deals with the history of marxism-leninism and the conflict between the marxist philosophers and other thinkers: Wittgenstein, Heidegger, Jaspers, Marcel, Camus, Berdyaev, Maritain and Harrington, representing neo-positivism, existentialism, neo-thomism and personalism.[4]

Apart from the common area of political education the curricula in all fields consist of two cycles: the first period of three to three and a half years is devoted to a more general kind of study; the second is spent upon the mastering of more specialised knowledge. A student of chemistry, therefore, takes inorganic, physical and analytical chemistry, mathematics, physics and other subjects in the first cycle and in the second may specialise in, for example, radio-chemistry, chemistry of proteins or polymers.

Students' progress is regularly assessed during their studies with the help of homework assignments, tests, end-of-term examinations and work in the laboratories. The student must pass all his examinations at the end of each term; those who fail can, however, try again after the vacations.

The diploma project or diploma thesis is a rigorous and independent study of an aspect of the student's special field of study. The theme of the project must be approved by the head of the department. The study and the writing of the thesis takes several months of work under the guidance of the student's scientific adviser. When the thesis is ready, the student has to present it to the university and defend it in an oral examination before a board of examiners consisting of the professors and the representatives from the Ministry. If the student is successful in defending his thesis he is awarded the graduate qualification, that is, a diploma.

Graduates are assigned jobs by a state commission which includes university members and Ministry officials, on the basis of the requirements presented to the various ministries by industrial enterprises and other units of production and passed on to the universities.

Each university is headed by a rector appointed by the Ministry, who is the chairman of the university senate, consisting of deans of faculties, professors who are heads of departments, the librarian and a number of representatives of public organisations connected with the university. Each university has also a vice-rector. Deans are elected by the professors of the particular faculty and their positions must be confirmed by the Ministry. All professors appointed to a chair must possess a Doctor's degree, all lecturers a Candidate's degree. About a quarter of the lecturers, but only about 5 per cent of the professors, are women.

The professors both teach and carry on with their research work. Their teaching load is normally ten hours per week. Lecturers normally teach or lead seminar work and laboratory work twelve hours per week, spending more time on preparation and research, often team-research.

The remuneration of the academic staff shows considerable differences depending upon the position. Assistants may receive between 170 and 280 roubles per month; lecturers (*dotsents*) between 270 and 320 roubles per month; professors between 400 and 500 roubles per month. Deans of faculties receive the professorial salary plus 35 per cent. The salary scales are subject to review from time to time.[5]

The University of Moscow   The University of Moscow was founded in 1755 on the initiative and according to the plan of a famous Russian scientist, Mikhail Lomonosov. In the more distant past many famous Russian writers, philosophers and reformers studied here: V. G. Belinsky, A. I. Herzen, N. P. Ogarev, N. I. Pirogov, K. A. Timiryazev and many others. Its scientific faculties occupy an impressive modern building in Lenin Hills, thirty-four storeys high, and erected between 1949 and 1953.

In 1967 Moscow University had fourteen faculties and 223

G

chairs. The faculties included the following: mathematics and mechanics, physics, chemistry, geology, geography, biology, economics, philosophy, law, history, psychology, philology, oriental studies and journalism. The University possessed four research institutes, 250 laboratories, 163 study rooms, 10 research centres, 3 museums, 4 observatories and a botanical garden. The staff numbered nearly 4,000 persons, including professors, lecturers and scientific workers. Among them were 35 full members and 44 corresponding members of the Academy of Sciences of the USSR, 500 Doctors of Science and over 1,800 Candidates of Science. Famous Soviet scientists, the physicists A. Stoletov, P. Lebedev, N. Umov, the chemists N. Zelinsky and A. Nesmeyanov, the experts in aerodynamics N. Zhukovsky and S. Chaplygin, the mathematicians A. Kolmogorov, I. Petrovsky and P. Aleksandrov, have taught in Moscow University.

The student body in 1969 exceeded 32,000, of whom 18,000 were full-time day students. More than sixty nationalities were represented. Some 6,000 students were accommodated in the university halls of residence. For every two adjacent bed-sitting rooms, each for one student, there is a bathroom. Each room has a divan, a book-case, a desk, a table and two chairs. There are one or two kitchens on each floor, but regular meals are taken in a university canteen.[6]

The University of Leningrad   St Petersburg University was founded on 20 February 1819, through the reorganisation of the Central Pedagogical Institute. At that time the University consisted of three faculties: philosophy and law, history and philology, and physics and mathematics; a fourth, the faculty of oriental studies, was added in 1854. The greatest Russian writers, thinkers and scientists studied here (I. S. Turgenev, D. I. Pisarev, K. S. Kalinovsky, N. G. Chernyshevsky, I. P. Pavlov) or taught here (D. I. Mendeleyev, E. H. Lentz, I. M. Sechenov, N. E. Vvedensky, A. A. Inostrantsev, A. N. Veselovsky, A. A. Shakhmatov, M. M. Kovalevsky). In 1891 Lenin took his examinations here and received a degree in the faculty of law.

The University consists of fourteen faculties: mathematics and mechanics, physics, chemistry, geology, geography, biology and

Table *13*
History Curriculum

No/Subject	Number	of	Hours
	Total	Lecture	Seminars and practical studies
1 *2*	*3*	*4*	*5*
1. History of the CPSU	220	120	100
2. Political economy	214	114	100
3. Dialectical and historical materialism	140	80	60
4. History of philosophy	70	70	–
5. Logic	70	44	26
6. Psychology	36	20	16
7. Pedagogics	56	56	–
8. Methodology of teaching	60	40	20
9. Foreign language	270	–	270
10. Latin	200	–	200
11. Fundamentals of archaeology	36	36	–
12. History of primitive society and fundamentals of ethnography	36	36	–
13. History of the ancient world	204	136	68
14. History of the Middle Ages	154	104	50
15. History of the Southern and Western Slavs	100	100	–
16. History of foreign Eastern countries (Middle Ages, modern, and current)	238	238	–
17. Modern and current history	300	200	100
18. History of the USSR	472	272	200
19. Russian language	36	–	36
20. Physical training and sports	136	–	136
21. Optional subjects	500	300	200
22. Pedagogical practice	6 weeks		
23. Production training	5 weeks		
24. Diploma work	Second term of fifth year		

Source: Prokofiev, M. A., and others. *Higher Education in the USSR* (Paris 1961), 44.

soil sciences, economics, philosophy, law, psychology, history, language and literature, oriental studies and journalism. There are 153 departments. In addition to the departments within the various faculties there are also some departments which are not attached to faculties, among them the departments of the history of the CPSU and of physical education. With the exception of the faculty of oriental studies all faculties have evening courses of study, and nine faculties offer courses by correspondence.

In January 1969 there were 1,829 persons on the teaching staff, of whom 281 had the degree of Doctor of Science and 811 the degree of Candidate of Science. Twenty-six members of the university staff were members or candidate members of the Academy of Sciences of the USSR.

On 1 January 1969 there were 19,064 students, of whom 10,029 were full-time day students, 5,046 were evening students and 3,989 were studying by correspondence; 72 per cent of the students received government grants and over 5,000 students from outside Leningrad were accommodated in the university hostels.

In 1969 there were eight scientific research institutes and several laboratories as well as a botanical garden, an observatory and a research station on the banks of the river Vorskla.

In the period 1970–80 a large university town is to be built in the suburbs of Leningrad, at Old Peterhof, to which the whole of the University will eventually be transferred.[7]

Polytechnic and specialised higher education institutes
Higher education establishments other than the universities consist of a small number of polytechnic institutes and over 700 monotechnic institutes for agriculture, medicine, pedagogy, economics, law, arts and physical culture.

The polytechnic institutes are large and well-known establishments training technologists in a large number of specialisations. The Leningrad Polytechnic Institute possesses ten faculties (including the evening and correspondence faculties) and trains specialists in forty-eight specialisations; the Kharkov Polytechnic Institute has fifteen faculties and teaches thirty-eight specialisations; the Urals Polytechnic Institute has thirteen faculties and teaches thirty-six specialisations; the Kaunas Polytechnic Institute has seven faculties and trains students in eighteen specialisations.

Over 200 monotechnic institutes prepare specialists in a particular branch of industry, construction, transport and communications. Some are well-known institutions, such as the Dnepropetrovsk Institute of Mining, the Moscow Power Institute, the Novosibirsk Building Institute, the Leningrad Electrotechnical Institute, the Rostov Institute of Agricultural Mechanical Engineering, the Magnitogorsk Mining and Metallurgical Institute, the Tashkent Textile Institute, the Rostov and Kharkov Institutes of Railway Engineering, the Kiev and Kuibyshev Institutes of Constructional Engineering.

There are almost one hundred agricultural institutes, training specialists for different branches of agriculture and forestry. They are spread all over the country and in their work they take regional needs into account: among them are the Armenian, Bashkir, Dagestan, Dnepropetrovsk, Zhitomir, Kirov, Crimean, Orenburg and Tashkent Agricultural Institutes, and the Archangelsk, Byelorussian, Voronezh and Urals Forestry Institutes. Some are highly specialised, for example the Azov and Chelyabinsk Institutes of Agricultural Mechanisation and Electrification. There are other institutes specialising in stock breeding and veterinary science.

Over eighty medical institutes train over 25,000 doctors a year in different specialisations: general medicine, pediatrics, public health, stomatology or pharmaceutics. The courses last six years. The most famous of these medical institutes are at Archangelsk, Bashkir, Voronezh, Gorky, Dagestan, Kazan, Minsk, Perm, Samarkand, Khabarovsk, Sverdlovsk and Smolensk.

Other institutes train economists, lawyers, actors, musicians, physical education experts and teachers. The latter are described in the section on teacher training. New institutes of every kind come into being every year to provide the economy with highly qualified experts in the field of applied science and technology.

The rules for admission of students, content of studies, teaching methods and internal organisation of the specialised higher education establishments are very similar to those obtaining in the universities.[8]

Higher degrees and academic titles   A unified system of certification of scientific and teaching personnel has been in existence in the USSR since 1934. There are two academic scientific degrees: Candidate of Science (*Kandidat nauk*) in, for instance, economics, mathematics, philosophy, physics, and Doctor of Science (*Doktor nauk*).

A graduate working for a Candidate's degree must finish the required higher education course extending over at least three years, pass examinations according to a special programme, write and publicly defend a thesis at a university or a research institution operating under the Academy of Sciences. The thesis must be published in advance.

To take the degree of Doctor of Science, the student must carry out extensive research and write a doctoral thesis on an accepted subject. After publication the thesis must be submitted by the author to the academic council of one of the higher education establishments or scientific institutes empowered to consider doctorate awards. The decision of the academic council to confer a degree upon the candidate is taken by a secret vote and has to be approved by the Higher Certification Commission of the Ministry of Higher and Secondary Specialised Education of the USSR.

The number of higher degrees awarded every year has increased enormously during recent times. In 1950, 4,093 persons obtained a Candidate's degree; in 1960, 5,517, in 1969, 25,810. Only about one Doctor's degree is awarded for every ten Candidate's degrees.

The following academic titles exist at the universities and higher education establishments: professor, senior lecturer (*dotsent*) and assistant lecturer (*assistent*). The titles in the research centres and institutes are: junior scientific worker (*mladshii nauchnyi sotrudnik*) and senior scientific worker (*starshii nauchnyi sotrudnik*). The title of assistant lecturer or junior scientific worker is conferred on persons with higher education, possessing the necessary qualifications and working under the guidance of a professor or a senior lecturer or a senior scientific worker. The title of senior lecturer or senior scientific worker is usually conferred on persons having a Candidate's degree and conducting appropriate teaching or research. The title of professor is conferred upon persons having a Doctor's degree and conducting extensive teaching or research.

ADULT EDUCATION

Educational opportunities for adults in the USSR involve a large number of institutions of different kinds, including a number which have already been described (evening and correspondence courses in secondary specialised and higher education). Other forms of adult education embrace parents' universities, universities of culture and libraries, and in the past included centres for the liquidation of illiteracy and the workers' faculties. The latter have recently been revived in a number of large industrial towns to prepare young and talented workers for full-time higher education. Industrial training constitutes a separate category. Also involved in adult education but primarily outside industry are the CPSU, state agencies of different kinds and the trade unions.

The general aim of educational-cultural work for adults is to increase communist consciousness and political activity in the great mass of the population, to raise the level of general culture and education and to promote the spirit of collectivism and love of work.

Parents' universities (*Roditelskie universitety*) The so-called parents' universities consist of series of lectures given in schools and workers' clubs for the benefit of parents, to improve their knowledge on the education and upbringing of their children. Attendance is voluntary and parents who attend have an opportunity to acquaint themselves with the different aspects of individual growth and development, child physiology, child psychology, school organisation and school work. The immediate objectives of the lectures are to prepare parents for taking an active part and playing a more positive role in parent-teacher associations and in parents' committees at school, and also to prepare some parents as effective leaders of circles of various kinds, operating in the schools on extra-curricular basis.

Universities of culture (*Universitety kultury*)   The universities of culture are a form of public education sponsored by the houses and palaces of culture, workers' clubs and factory clubs. There is no set programme of activities. The prospective students themselves decide on the nature of the course and its length. In general, lectures and discussions are held on literature, art, theatre and cinema, music, science and education. Lectures are often followed by visits to theatres, concerts, museums and art galleries. Occasionally there are talks by writers, poets, composers, actors or film producers. There are no tests or examinations and only nominal fees are charged to the participants.

It is also important to remember that both the Soviet radio and television networks regularly broadcast educational programmes of various kinds, while a very extensive system of libraries operates throughout the country and provides the background facilities to the universities of culture.

Schools for Working and Rural Youth (*Shkoly Rabochey i Selskoy Molodyozhi*)   The Schools for Working and Rural Youth are educational establishments offering part-time education in the evening or, exceptionally, during the day for shift workers, at secondary general education level, on a voluntary basis, for all young people who for one reason or another have not been able to obtain it so far. Normally, it applies to those who have finished the eight-year schools and now want to complete their secondary education on a part-time basis without giving up employment. There are, however, also facilities for those who have only finished some of the lower grades and need first of all to cover the material of the eight-year school.

The extent of demand for this kind of education can be seen from Table 14.

The decreasing demand for education in the lower grades is obviously due to the existence of universal compulsory education up to fifteen since 1958, while the almost three-fold increase in the numbers studying in the ninth, tenth and eleventh grades in the last decade is clearly due to the advantages and increased

Table 14

Numbers of Schools for Working and Rural Youth and their Students

	1950/51	1960/61	1969/70
Number of schools*	20,465	25,229	16,971
Number of students†	1,438	2,770	4,041
in grades 1 to 4	352	54	45
5 to 8	894	1,655	1,005
9 to 11	192	1,061	2,991

* Including primary, incomplete secondary and complete secondary schools at which exist classes for working and rural youth and independent correspondence schools.

† In thousands, including correspondence students.

Source: Tsentralnoe Statisticheskoe Upravlenie. *Narodnoe khozyaystvo SSSR v 1969 g.* (Moscow 1970), 667.

opportunities for further study and promotion which one can derive from completing a full course of secondary education.

The Schools for Working and Rural Youth came into existence on the basis of the 1943 law on the Education of the Young People Working in Enterprises and the 1944 law on the Organisation of Evening Schools for Rural Youth. They were reformed and reorganised on the basis of the 1958 law and their present work and organisation are based upon the Statute on the Evening (Shift) Secondary School of General Education approved by the Council of Ministers of the RSFSR on 29 December 1959.

Schools of this type may be opened in towns, working settlements and rural districts by decision of the Council of Ministers of autonomous republics or of the executive committees of territorial, regional or municipal (in the case of Moscow and Leningrad) councils of workers' deputies. They remain under the authority of the district or municipal department of public education. If there are a sufficient number of pupils, such schools may also be set up at industrial and transport enterprises, on building sites, state farms, collective farms and repair stations. If there are not enough pupils for opening a separate independent evening school, individual classes may be set up in secondary education labour polytechnic schools.

Depending upon the actual conditions in which the pupils are working the courses of instruction may be held in the evening or daytime (for shift workers) or may be concentrated in the periods of time when the pupils are free from work (eg, seasonal variations in work in agriculture, in the river fleet enterprises).

In the Schools for Working and Rural Youth pupils study the same range of general subjects and are given the same basic education and skills as in full-time secondary schools. Twenty hours a week are devoted to study, including fifteen hours of class work, three hours of individual consultations and two hours of optional studies to improve the pupils' vocational qualifications; 33 per cent of teaching time is devoted to the study of literature, history, the USSR constitution, economic geography and a foreign language; 42 per cent to the study of natural and exact sciences, including mathematics, astronomy, physics, chemistry, biology and technical drawing; 10 per cent to the options and 15 per cent to individual consultations. The teaching methods used make allowances for the special type of pupil attending the school, in that they have industrial experience and a more mature outlook upon life.

A shortened working week or a shortened working day is granted to pupils studying in the ninth, tenth and eleventh grades, and twenty days' additional leave with pay is given before the final examination in grade eleven.

Each school is headed by a suitably qualified director appointed by the Ministry of Education of the autonomous republic or the territorial or regional department of public education. The director guides the work of the school, directs the activities of the student body and maintains close contact with the Party, the trade unions and the Komsomol. However, since the pupils of the evening schools are members of the Party, trade union or Komsomol organisations in the factories or on the farms where they work, these organisations are not set up within this kind of school.

The teachers are appointed by the district or municipal department of public education and are responsible for the quality of instruction in each subject they teach. A pedagogical council must be established in each school to keep under review the links between school work and production and the quality of education in the school.

In each school there is also a pupils' council which consists of the pupils' representatives from each grade, whose function it is to unite the pupils into a closely knit group and to direct their activities to the general improvement of the school's work.[9]

Industrial training Training in industry, in the form of special facilities both for training new workers and improving the qualifications of the existing labour force in an industrial establishment, is one of the most interesting and characteristic features of the Soviet economy. It involves millions of workers, who consider it their duty to strive constantly for the improvement of their technical qualifications. Because of the system of industrial grading and widespread payment by results it is also to the personal advantage of a worker.

Theoretical training is closely connected with production work. The workers study and learn in the same place, usually a large industrial enterprise. The present pattern has emerged on the basis of long experience of such enterprises as the Likhachov Motor Works in Moscow, the Leningrad Metallurgical Works and the Rostov Agricultural Machinery Works. The organisation of training is in the hands of the Department of Technical Education of a given enterprise. It is an independent department, directly subordinated to the management, and consists of six or more persons, including engineer-instructors in methods, who direct the training and control its content and quality. The department prepares long and short-term plans for training workers and appoints instructors from the most experienced and the best-qualified workers, engineers and technicians.

Separate accommodation is available in the plant in the form of study rooms for theoretical instruction in, for example, machine construction, metal technology or technical drawing. The study rooms are equipped with teaching aids, such as models, component parts of machines and other equipment, diagrams and technical drawings.

New, unqualified workers are assigned after registration to fully qualified worker-instructors for practical training, and

simultaneously are put into groups for theoretical training. The
resultant training aims at supplying trainees with all the necessary
industrial skills and theoretical knowledge in accordance with the
statutory requirements set out in the reference books on skill-
grading. The trainee is then prepared for the vocational examination in a specific specialisation. Production training is conducted
according to a prescribed programme directly on-the-job; in
general it includes the learning of safety techniques, preparing
equipment for work, work training under supervision, independent work and the final qualifying tests. Theoretical work proceeds according to the programmes for occupational and technical
training prepared and approved by the State Committee for
Vocational-Technical Education of the USSR Council of
Ministers.

After the completion of the full course the trainee has to pass
the examination before the qualifying commission. He is examined on any matters included in the course of training and has
samples of his qualifying work assessed. The commission prepares a report on the results of the examination and issues the
trainee with a certificate. On the basis of the report instructions
are issued to the workshop where the newly qualified worker is to
be employed concerning the award to the worker of the appropriate qualification and industrial category. If the trainee fails the
examination, he has the right to present himself for another test
in two weeks' time.

The courses for the improvement of the qualifications of the
existing industrial personnel are conducted through industrial-
technical courses, special-purpose courses and courses for learning advanced methods of production.

Industrial-technical courses are organised for the workers who
have already learnt their occupations and have worked in their
specialisation for no less than a year. In their daily work performance is naturally improved through practice, but often the
mastering of new skills becomes imperative. Financial incentives
also play a role, as earnings depend upon the qualifications
acquired and the more highly skilled work that goes with them.

In these courses the training methods are similar to those used in the training of new workers, and both production and theoretical training are involved. The duration of this type of course varies, and depends upon the specialisation: the more complex it is, the longer the training. Theoretical instruction takes place usually two or three times per week, while practical work proceeds parallel with it. Successful completion of the course leads to the award of a higher category of industrial qualification.

The special-purpose courses serve to acquaint the worker with any new aspects of production: the introduction of a new technological process, new equipment, new methods in processing component parts, raw or intermediate materials. The training is conducted by engineers and technicians specially chosen for the purpose, and already familiar with the new techniques. The workers are organised into groups of twenty. Practical training is conducted in the workshops; theoretical work is done during time taken out of work.

Courses for mastering the latest methods of production have increased in importance in recent years as a result of growing stress on improvements in industrial efficiency, in production and in productivity of labour. Courses of this type have been introduced on a large scale in order to popularise the methods and achievements of outstanding workers who have exceeded the set production norms, produced goods of better quality or who have successfully economised in the use of raw and intermediate materials, equipment and tools.

The latest methods of production are taught by the norm-setters, the technologists and other specialists who work out the best ways for teaching such methods and the most effective ways for popularising them among workers. During the training, a small number of learners are attached to the instructing worker or specialist, who is often assisted by a consultant from among the technologists or engineers. The training takes place on-the-job. If necessary, the consultant may also conduct theoretical work. The training normally lasts not longer than a month. It is considered as accomplished when the learners have completely mastered the new methods and begin to achieve in their work results equal to those produced by their instructor-demonstrators.

The consequence is an improvement in productivity which, according to recent experience, may on average be in the region of 10–15 per cent.

Quite apart from the above, courses have also been instituted for learning a second, related occupation, or mastering a different, new specialisation. This has been found necessary because of changing techniques, the growing complexity of modern equipment and the introduction of advanced mechanisation and automation in modern industrial production. In addition, the character of production sometimes makes the mastering of more than one specialisation by one worker necessary if maximum productivity is to be achieved. As a result the Soviet worker, far from resisting the idea of a second specialisation or occupation, willingly combines new skills with the old ones. In consequence fully qualified turners become also qualified milling-machine operators, capstan operators become also tool setters, maintenance men become fitters and electric welders become also oxyacetylene welders.

It should also be kept in mind that many young workers, specially in larger towns, attend evening courses in higher or secondary specialised education establishments, study by correspondence or are sent by their enterprise to study full-time.

The departments of industrial training in factories and works of different kinds sometimes also act as agencies helping pupils from the last two grades of complete secondary schools to do their labour training in the form of an industrial practice in the enterprise.[10]

Notes to chapter 4 are on p 128

5
Teacher Education and Status

TEACHER TRAINING

THE training of teachers in the USSR was carried out in the academic year 1969/70 at 205 pedagogic institutes, 49 state universities and 411 pedagogic schools. In the academic year 1966/7 there were 206 pedagogic institutes and 386 pedagogic schools. In the period 1966–70 6 new pedagogic institutes were opened, 2 were closed and 5 were reorganised into universities. In the same period 25 new pedagogic schools came into existence.[1]

The different types of teacher training establishments all aim at preparing teachers for the various types of schools in the country, from the kindergartens to the upper secondary schools. The unifying element behind the different types of teacher training institutions is the concept of a teacher:

> The Soviet teacher is first and foremost an ideological educator, responsible for developing among young people a scientific, social, political and civic outlook. To be equal to this task, the teacher, in addition to receiving a thorough specialised and professional training, should acquire a broad philosophical and socio-political outlook.[2]

Pedagogic schools (*Pedagogicheskie uchilishcha*)   The training of teachers for primary schools had been conducted in pre-revolutionary Russia in the teachers' seminaries which were subsequently transformed into pedagogic technicums by the Soviet authorities. They offered a four-year course to the pupils who completed the seven-year school. These were reformed in 1937 to become pedagogic schools and again in 1954, to accept students with ten-year secondary education for a two-year course.

In the 1950s plans were made to make teacher training at all levels a part of higher education and to gradually phase out the pedagogic schools as secondary specialised education establishments. In fact, the number of pedagogic schools went down from 755 in the academic year 1950/1 to 625 in 1955/6 and even further to 404 in 1960/1; it began to grow again and it was 468 in 1964/5, when it began to decrease once more, only to show a tendency to increase again in the period 1967–70. The number of students studying in the pedagogic schools both full-time and part-time was 300,000 in the academic year 1965/6 and 342,000 in 1969/70. About 50,000 to 60,000 students graduate annually from the pedagogic schools offering full-time education.[3]

The 411 pedagogic schools today admit students with a full secondary education and train them for two years as teachers for kindergartens and the primary grades, as well as students with eight years of schooling whom they train for three and a half years if they want to teach in a kindergarten, or for four years if they want to teach the primary grades. Each pedagogic school normally has, therefore, a faculty preparing teachers for pre-school establishments and other faculties preparing teachers for grades one to four (in the future one to three—see p 27).

The curriculum includes general education subjects, specialist subjects, pedagogic subjects and practical training. The general subjects include social studies, mathematics, physics, chemistry, geography, biology, a foreign language and scientific atheism. The specialist subjects consist of the study of Russian language and literature, arithmetic, nature study, history, music, drawing and physical education, together with the corresponding methods. Pedagogic subjects include psychology, pedagogy, anatomy, physiology and hygiene. Practical training consists principally of school workshop practice. Teaching practice is an important part of the programme and it is confined to the second half of the course, but a primary school is normally attached to a pedagogic school and observing qualified teachers at work starts earlier. The students are required to prepare their own teaching aids and to learn to play at least one musical instrument. The details of the curriculum for a four-year course can be seen from Table 15.

Table 15
Pedagogic School Curriculum (*Primary Teaching*)

	I		II		III		IV		Total
Year: / Semester:	1	2	1	2	1	2	1	2	hours
General Subjects:									
Social studies							2	3	81
Mathematics	2	2	2	3	3	3	3	4	398
Physics and astronomy	2	2	2	2	2	2	2	2	294
Chemistry	3	2	3	2					194
Economic geography								4	60
Biology							2	2	66
Foreign language	3	2	2	2					175
Scientific atheism								1	15
Total general subjects	10	8	9	9	5	5	9	16	1,283
Specialist Subjects:									
Russian language and methods	3	3	2	4	4	3	4	3	479
Literature	4	2	3	2	3	2	3	3	403
Arithmetic and methods	4	4	4	2	2	2			344
Nature study and methods		2	2	3					138
History and methods	3	2	2	2	3	2			266
Anatomy, physiology, hygiene	2	2							78
Psychology		4							80
Pedagogy			5	4	2	2			247
Singing and methods	2	2	2	2	2	2	2	2	294
Drawing/modelling and methods	2	2	2	2	2	2	2	2	294
Theory and method of PE					2	2	1		90
Educational materials	1			1		1	1	4	134
Total specialist subjects	21	23	22	22	20	18	13	14	2,847
Physical education	2	2	2	2	2	2	2	2	294
Civil defence							1	1	33
School workshop training	2	2	2	2	2	2	2	2	294
Agricultural studies, etc	1	1	1	1	1	1	1	1	147
Technical media						2	2		70
Teaching practice					6	6	6		324
Total hours	36	36	36	36	36	36	36	36	5,292

Optional subjects not included
Continuous teaching practice and pioneer camp practice: 10 weeks

Source: N. Grant. 'Teacher Training in the USSR and Eastern Europe', Comparative Education Society of Europe, British Section, *Trends in Teacher Education* (1970), 72.

H

At the end of their course of study the students take the final examination and are awarded their kindergarten or primary school teacher diploma. An overwhelming majority of the students in pedagogic schools are girls and practically all receive state scholarships.

Pedagogic institutes (*Pedagogicheskie instituty*)   Pedagogic institutes constitute the most important source of supply of teachers in the USSR. Every fourth higher education establishment is a pedagogic institute and about one-quarter of all higher education students study in the pedagogic institutes.

The 205 pedagogic institutes had in the academic year 1969/70 over 850,000 students studying full-time, in evening courses or by correspondence. The latter two forms of study are very popular; only about 70,000 teachers graduate annually from the full-time courses in pedagogic institutes.

The pedagogic institutes train teachers for all grades. Courses lasting five years (since 1956) prepare teachers for all subjects in grades five to ten. The courses preparing teachers for pre-school establishments and the first four grades last four years. Each institute has several faculties corresponding to the different subjects.

The minimum entrance qualification is the completion of a full course of secondary education. A competitive entrance examination eliminates, however, two out of every three candidates for admission.

The curriculum consists of socio-political, special and pedagogic subjects. The first group includes the history of the CPSU, political economy, philosophy and scientific communism. The study of the special subject occupies the central place and includes numerous subdivisions of it. The pedagogic subjects consist of psychology, educational theory, history of education and school hygiene. The course in educational theory has three parts. The first is devoted to general issues: the subject and methods of education; the aims and tasks of education; development and education; the aims and content of intellectual, moral, aesthetic, physical and vocational education; the characteristic features of the systems of education in the USSR and abroad. The second part is devoted to didactics and covers the study of the nature of the teaching process, the principles, forms and methods of teaching, including the fundamentals of programmed learning. The third part concentrates on the study of the forms and methods of educational work in out-of-school activities and pupils' organisations, the education of children at home, and so on.

The theoretical material is presented in the form of lectures and supplemented by reading. Seminar work involves the presentation of reports and papers upon educational problems of all kinds by individual students and a general discussion on the issues raised by the group.

Teaching practice plays an important role. This involves the students acting as helpers in the extra-curricular activities in the schools during the first and second year of study. In the summer they act as leaders in the Young Pioneer camps. During the last two years of study, teaching practice is organised in schools under the guidance of methodologists, lecturers in the institute and experienced schoolteachers.

A really determined effort has recently been made by the Ministry of Higher and Secondary Specialised Education to prepare and introduce new syllabuses into the institutes. In the academic year 1970/1 new syllabuses came into force in the following subjects: Russian (or native) language and literature, mathematics, physics, history, foreign languages, biology, chemistry, pedagogy, pre-school psychology, music and singing and physical education.

Table 16 represents a typical curriculum in the pedagogic institute (see p 116).

Most of the pedagogic institutes nowadays prepare teachers of one subject. Only a few train teachers to teach two subjects. The students must present regular written work (*zachety*) and longer papers (*kursovye raboty*). Each student must pass the internal institute examination and four state examinations. One of these is in the history of the CPSU and the other three vary, depending upon specialisation.

After obtaining the diploma, the students are allocated jobs in schools, the best usually being able to obtain positions in

Table 16

Pedagogic Institute Curriculum (Russian Language and Literature)

	Year: I		II		III		IV		
Semester:	1	2	1	2	1	2	1	2	Total
History of the CPSU	3	4							120
Marxist-leninist philosophy			4	3					120
Political economy					2	0/4			80
Scientific communism							2	3	70
Psychology	2	2							74
Pedagogy			2	3					80
History of pedagogy					2	0/2			60
School hygiene			1						20
Foreign language	4	4	2	2	2				240
Physical education	2	2	2	2					140
Introduction to linguistics	4								76
Old Slavonic	2	2							74
Dialectology		2							36
Historical grammar			3	2					86
Modern Russian language			6	6	6	2/6		2	420
History of literary language								3	42
Stylistics								3	42
General linguistics								4	56
Russian language method					3	0/2			80
Literature method					2	0/1			50
Practical work in Russian	3	3							110
Introduction to literary theory	3								60
Russian and Soviet literature	3	3	3	4	6	4/4	2	4	500
Literary theory								4	28
Foreign literature	2	2	2	3	3	2/4			270
Elective subjects					4	4/5	4	3	280
Subjects determined by republic	2	6	5	5					300
Total hours	30	30	30	30	30	12/28	8	24	3,514

Optional courses not included

Pioneer camp and continuous teaching practice: 30 weeks

Source: N. Grant. 'Teacher Training in the USSR and Eastern Europe', Comparative Education Society of Europe, British Section, *Trends in Teacher Education* (1970), 74.

areas of their choice. This does not, by any means, apply to all students.

Most institutes possess evening and correspondence faculties offering these kinds of training to the young men and women who are studying without interrupting full-time employment. There are two independent pedagogic institutes, in Moscow and Erevan, the capital of Armenia, which provide teacher training exclusively by correspondence. Training of this kind covers the same subjects and possesses the same character as in the full-time study, but the course lasts two years longer. Predominant among those who study in the evening or by correspondence are the teachers of primary grades, the teachers of grades five to eight who have not completed their higher education, teachers who want to gain qualifications to teach other subjects, kindergarten teachers and Young Pioneer leaders. Competitive entrance examinations are also held for the evening and correspondence faculties, and those who graduate from these faculties enjoy exactly the same rights as those who have graduated from the day faculties.

The pedagogic institutes also accept students for full-time advanced courses leading to higher degrees. A course of study and research leading to the award of the degree of Candidate of Pedagogic Sciences lasts three years on a full-time basis, or a year longer on a part-time basis after the award of the diploma.

Universities About 15–20 per cent of the new teachers starting their work in the Soviet schools every year come from the universities. The actual proportion of university graduates going into teaching varies, however, very much from one faculty to another. Over 90 per cent of Russian language and literature graduates go into teaching; 85 per cent of history graduates; about 50 per cent of geographers and 35 per cent of biologists but only 25 per cent of mathematics and physics graduates and 20 per cent of foreign language specialists.[4]

University students are trained for both scientific research and teaching. By comparison with the students in pedagogic institutes, they receive a narrower but more specialised training in a particular branch of learning and undertake research on a much wider scale. The political subjects receive great emphasis but

pedagogic subjects and teaching methods are given less importance in the universities. The courses in psychology and theory
of education are shorter, school hygiene is not taught and there
is less teaching practice in schools.

Recently, due to the increasing numbers of pupils staying on
at school to seventeen and to the introduction of specialised
options in the upper grades, the demand for university trained
teachers has increased. As a result some of the universities have
established teacher-training departments where students who
want to become teachers may be separately enrolled.[5]

**Institutes for the Improvement of Teachers' Qualifica-
tions**   Special institutes exist in the regions, territories and
autonomous republics for the explicit purpose of improving the
professional qualifications of practising teachers. This is done
through regular refresher courses and advisory services. Teachers
are invited to attend a refresher course in their specialisation once
every four or five years in order to acquaint themselves with
recent developments and progress in their subjects as well as with
new teaching techniques. Some of the larger institutes, for
example the Moscow Institute for the Improvement of Teachers'
Qualifications, opened in 1938, are organised into departments,
each dealing with one particular subject of the school curriculum.
The courses are conducted by professors and lecturers from
the universities or pedagogical institutes, directors of schools
and teachers with long experience in their own fields. Teachers
attend on a particular day of the week for each of the different
subjects.

In addition, the institutes for the improvement of teachers'
qualifications organise consultations on all subjects, seminars and
special lectures on teaching problems and may issue pamphlets
and booklets to popularise new ideas and improvements.

Similar services for practising teachers are also offered by many
universities, pedagogic institutes or specialised higher education
establishments of other kind.

Pedagogical readings (*Pedagogicheskie chteniya*)   The general level of pedagogical knowledge and teaching standards among
the practising teachers is also being raised with the help of

pedagogical societies which hold the popular pedagogical readings, with the assistance of pedagogic institutes, institutes for the improvement of teachers' qualifications and the Academy of Pedagogical Sciences.

Pedagogical readings take the form of conferences at the national, republican, district or city level, during which reports are presented by a number of outstanding pedagogues, experts in method, and innovators. The authors of such reports, which often contain the description and analysis of valuable teaching experiences, are awarded cash prizes and diplomas. The most valuable reports are chosen for publication.

The popularity of pedagogical readings is increasing and competition for the privilege of reading a report is growing among teachers, lecturers and research workers. In 1965 over 10,000 papers were submitted for the central pedagogical readings of the RSFSR, of which 3,000 were selected.

The pedagogical societies of the different union republics are important associations gathering educational experts, school teachers, institute and university lecturers and professors. According to the statistics, the Pedagogical Society of the RSFSR had 228,000 members in 1966.[6]

THE STATUS OF TEACHERS

Remuneration   The remuneration of teachers and administrative workers in education is fixed by law. The average monthly rates of pay for teachers in the schools of general education were last fixed by a law adopted by the Supreme Soviet of the USSR in July 1964, when they were increased by an average of 25 per cent, with a more substantial increase for the teachers in primary schools. Since that year the rate of pay for a teacher with higher education teaching grades one to ten and up to five years' experience has been 80 roubles per month; for a teacher in a similar position with five to ten years' experience—90 roubles; with ten to twenty-five years' experience—100 roubles; with more than twenty-five years' experience—137 roubles.[7]

The remuneration of a teacher teaching primary grades is based upon four hours of teaching per day, or twenty-four hours per week. The remuneration of the teachers of higher grades is based upon three hours of teaching per day, or eighteen hours per week. Additional teaching hours are paid extra. Teachers correcting pupils' written work in Russian, a native language or a foreign tongue, literature and mathematics receive an additional 6 roubles per month. There are also additional payments for a teacher in charge of a laboratory or of a library, if there is no librarian in the school. Teachers in the Far North territories receive supplementary allowances after the expiration of the statutory term of service. Teachers in rural areas receive free living quarters, lighting and heating and plots of ground for a garden.

Salaries and rules concerning the remuneration of teachers and instructors in the secondary specialised and vocational-technical schools are very similar to those for teachers in secondary general education schools.

The salaries of the administrators in the educational system, that is of directors, vice-directors and heads of departments, are determined by the length of service and the number of students or pupils in the establishment in which they work.[8]

It is of interest that the average monthly pay in the USSR was 90·8 roubles in 1964 and 116·9 roubles in 1969.[9] Teachers' pay is also to go up from 1 September 1972, by an average of about 20 per cent.

On retirement, teachers with at least twenty-five years of service receive a pension amounting to 40 per cent of their salary. The retirement age is sixty years of age for men and fifty-five for women.

In comparing the rates of pay of the Soviet teachers with those in other countries, it is important to remember that in the USSR the proportion of goods and services available to the population either free or at a subsidised price is higher than elsewhere. Soviet sources suggest that the value of such benefits, when translated into money terms, amounts to about a third of the average monthly pay.

The Trade Union of Workers in Education   The USSR Trade Union of Workers in Education, Higher Schools and

Scientific Establishments (*Profsoyuz Rabotnikov Prosveshcheniya, Vysshei Shkoly i Nauchnykh Uchrezhdenii SSSR*) combines in its ranks university lecturers and professors, kindergarten teachers and schoolteachers, as well as the auxiliary staff in all kinds of educational establishments. It is one of the larger unions, with more than 4 million members, of whom more than a half are schoolteachers. Membership is not obligatory, but practically all teachers are members. Union dues are fixed at $1\frac{1}{2}$ per cent of the members' salaries.

The Central Committee of the Union publishes jointly with the Ministry of Education of the USSR *The Teachers' Newspaper* (*Uchitelskaya Gazeta*). It comes out three times a week and contains official announcements concerning education, articles explaining administrative measures, reports on the work and achievements of particular schools and educational establishments and also letters to the editor, often written by persons seeking advice on professional matters. The paper was established in 1924 and its circulation today is 550,000 copies.

Social status and prestige of teachers   In the school year 1969/70 there were 2,608,000 teachers in all schools of general education in the USSR, of whom about 70 per cent were women.[10] Because of their importance in the process of rearing the communist man of the future, teachers are considered to be one of the most important groups in Soviet society. Well over 235,000 were decorated with medals and orders for long and successful service. About 19,000 outstanding teachers were awarded the honorary title of Merited Teacher of their republics. Several thousand were awarded honorary certificates from the All-Union Central Council of Trade Unions.

Schoolteachers take an active part in political life. Many are deputies of the USSR Supreme Soviet, and the Supreme Soviets of the Union and autonomous republics include numerous teachers.

It is clear that the teachers in the Soviet Union play a great role in raising the general standards of culture in the country and in their daily work are laying down the foundations for social and material progress. At the same time, in that political objectives cannot be dissociated from schoolwork in general, Soviet teachers consistently strengthen the political foundations upon which the whole system is based.

Notes to chapter 5 are on p 128

Conclusions

BEFORE looking towards the future of education in the USSR one should, perhaps, first look back upon the fifty-five years of educational progress in that country.

It is clear that in the course of a half-century great progress has been made at all levels and in all aspects of education. From a country which lagged behind the west of Europe as much educationally as it did economically, the USSR has moved to occupy an important place in the sphere of educational progress.

It has not been an even and upward trend for the whole of that period. Indeed, initially progress was slow and there were setbacks. Universal adult literacy was not achieved until World War II. Only by 1932 were nearly all children between eight and eleven years of age attending school. Even half a century was not long enough to attain the objectives set out at the Eighth Congress of the Communist Party in March 1919, of securing universal and compulsory education, both general and technical, for all children and young people of both sexes up to seventeen years of age. But the record of development of Soviet education is impressive enough to suggest that no other country accomplished as much in a similar period of time.

The key elements in the processes of expansion and improvement of education in the USSR have been the conviction that education was the crucial factor conditioning social and economic progress, and the general belief that to learn and to work was for each man and woman a matter of civic duty and not simply of personal advantage. Other features were equally significant. Soviet educational theory rejected the idea that intelligence was determined by hereditary influences or fixed at birth and asserted that it was dependent upon the environment, both physical and social. Marxist psychologists dismissed the hypothesis of the existence of inborn intellectual potential and character traits and expressed the belief that individual development was conditioned by education and environmental influences. This was a powerful argument of an egalitarian nature.

Another consideration is secular morality. The Soviet schools and youth organisations promote a system of values which is materialistic and secular. They are very intimately associated with the political objectives but within them there is an important element of traditional values of materialist philosophy, atheistic not agnostic.

The Soviet commitment to scientific and technological progress has constantly been stressed and has produced results. Higher education, secondary specialised education and vocational-technical education have been planned specifically to meet the needs of industry and the economy as a whole. The parallel processes of mechanisation, automation, electrification and industrialisation could have only been consistently sustained through such an orientation.

Above all there is the political commitment, permeating all educational institutions, from the kindergarten to the university, and all aspects of education and individual development. The transmission of values and fundamental attitudes, governing the application of knowledge which has been acquired, is intimately connected with the building of a communist society. Today, the political commitment is not weaker but stronger than it has ever been. There is no reason to suppose that it will weaken in the foreseeable future.

Some concrete problems awaiting solution in the near future can be indicated.

Compulsory universal general education up to the age of fifteen having been achieved, the exact nature of the post-compulsory, differentiated system of upper secondary education will have to be determined, so that the relationship between the different types of educational establishments at this level becomes clear. The problems of the basis of selection for the different types, the parity of status among them, the transferability of students, as well as the equivalence of their final qualifications, will not be easy to solve in a society where individual aspirations are beginning to play an important role.

The concept of polytechnic education must remain a consideration of the greatest importance for a society bound to the elimination of social distinction between mental and physical labour. The most effective kind of polytechnic education has not yet been determined, and probably cannot be until the industrialisation of the country has everywhere reached an advanced stage. In the meantime, local conditions must decide its character and scope.

Selection for higher education is also posing a dilemma. When almost all school leavers want to obtain higher education and there are places for no more than 20–25 per cent of the age group, how are the students to be selected? Only some 3–8 per cent of school leavers in large industrial towns intend to take up full-time employment straight away after leaving school; an overwhelming majority want to go on studying full-time. In the rural areas most of the school leavers have little desire to work on the land. In the urban areas the least favoured occupations are those of shop assistants, workers in municipal enterprises and clerks. The interests of the economy and individual preferences cannot be easily reconciled. Will compulsion or persuasion be applied? Will the competitive element in the system of selection be allowed to become even more competitive or can another solution be found? The problems facing Soviet education have become problems facing many other countries in the world also.

Demographic trends in the USSR reveal the features characteristic of an industrially developed country: a declining birthrate, low mortality rate, stable population growth, growing geographical and occupational mobility of the population. This is a stage where qualitative improvement replaces the quantitative expansion simply to cope with the rapidly growing numbers. The Soviet Union has for years been rigorously pursuing the policy of making the fullest possible use of the economic potential of the country, which is plainly enormous. It is clear that education has been and is being assigned a key role in this process. This, at least, should not escape anybody's attention.

Notes

Chapter *1* THE ROOTS OF THE SOVIET EDUCATIONAL SYSTEM

1   Fitzpatrick, Sheila. *The Commissariat of Enlightenment* (London 1970), 285.
2   Lane, David. *Politics and Society in the USSR* (London 1969), 65.
3   Bereday, George, and others. *The Changing Soviet School* (Boston 1960), 63.
4   Galkin, K. *The Training of Scientists in the Soviet Union* (Moscow 1959), 98.
5   Central Committee of the CPSU and the USSR Council of Ministers. *Bringing Soviet Schools Still Closer to Life*, Soviet Booklet No 44 (London 1958), 4.
6   Ibid, 7.
7   Nozhko, K., and others. *Educational Planning in the USSR* (Paris 1968), 38.
8   Twenty-second Congress of the CPSU. *The Programme of the Communist Party of the Soviet Union*, Soviet Booklet No 83 (London 1961), 81-2.
9   Nozhko, K., and others, 275.
10 Twenty-second Congress of the CPSU, 44.
11 Lane, David, 517.
12 Ibid, 518-19.
13 Agranovsky, I., and others. *USSR Questions and Answers* (Moscow, nd), 147-8.
14 Ibid, 43-66.
15 *Soviet News* No 5584 (London 1971), 98.
16 Tsentralnoe Statisticheskoe Upravlenie. *Narodnoe khozyaystvo SSSR v 1969 g.* (Moscow 1970), 30.
17 Ibid, 7.
18 Lane, David, 505-8.
19 Tsentralnoe Statisticheskoe Upravlenie, 537.
20 Ibid, 34-5.
21 *Soviet News* No 5584, 98.

22 Ibid, 97.
23 Ibid, 97.
24 *Soviet News* No 5526, 34.

Chapter 2 ADMINISTRATION, FINANCE AND PLANNING

1 Nozhko, K., and others, 227.
2 Ministry of Education of the USSR. *On the Main Trends in the Field of Education in the USSR in 1968–1970* (Moscow 1970), 25–7.
3 Ibid, 30–1.
4 Nozhko, K., 233.
5 Ministry of Education of the USSR. *Public Education in the Soviet Union in 1966/67* (Moscow 1967), 48.
6 Nozhko, K., 166–7.
7 Ibid, 282.
8 Ibid, 285.
9 Ibid, 81–3.
10 Ibid, 83–4.

Chapter 3 THE SCHOOL SYSTEM

1 Ministry of Education of the USSR. *On the Main Trends in the Field of Education in the USSR in 1968–1970*, 19.
2 Ibid, 21.
3 'Statutes of the General-Education School', *The Current Digest of the Soviet Press*, Volume XXII, 38 (Columbus 1970), 1–6.
4 Prokofiev, M. A., and others. *Narodnoe Obrazovanie v SSSR* (Moscow 1967), 306.
5 Kairov, I. A., and others. *Pedagogicheskii Slovar* (Moscow 1960), 741–2.
6 Lane, David, 174.
7 Tsentralnoe Statisticheskoe Upravlenie, 678.
8 Ibid, 551.
9 Nozhko, K., and others, 250–2.
10 Grant, Nigel. *Soviet Education* (London 1964), 166.
11 Ibid, 65.
12 Tsentralnoe Statisticheskoe Upravlenie, 675.
13 Brezhnev, Leonid. *Report of the Central Committee of the Communist Party of the Soviet Union* (Moscow 1971), 93–4.
14 Tyazhelnikov, E. *Otchet Ts.K. VLKSM i zadachi Komsomola po vospitaniyu molodyozhi v dukhe leninskikh zavetov* (Moscow 1970), 4–8, 22–7, 52–5.

Chapter 4   HIGHER AND ADULT EDUCATION

1   Grant, Nigel, 110.
2   Tsentralnoe Statisticheskoe Upravlenie, 676.
3   Nozhko, K., and others, 283.
4   Ministerstvo Vysshego i Srednego Spetsialnogo Obrazovaniya
     SSSR. *Programma Kursa Istorii Filosofii* (Moscow 1967), 7–51.
5   Nozhko, K., 283.
6   Agranovsky, I., and others, 356.
7   Shilov, L. A. *The University of Leningrad 1819–1969* (Leningrad
     1969), 3–28.
8   Nozhko, K., 124.
9   Shapovalenko, S. G., and others. *Polytechnical Education in the
     USSR* (Paris 1963), 413–22.
10 Plyasov, M. T. 'The Training of Personnel at the Moscow Light
     Car Plant', *Year Book of Education 1968* (London 1968), 271–85.

Chapter 5   TEACHER EDUCATION AND STATUS

1   Ministry of Education of the USSR. *On the Main Trends in the
     Field of Education in the USSR in 1968–1970*, 21.
2   Ogorodnikov, I. T. and Ilyina, T. A. 'Professional Preparation of
     Teachers in the Light of Recent Advances in Educational Theory
     and Teaching Techniques. Educational Development in the
     USSR', in Yates, Alfred, *Current Problems of Teacher Education*
     (Hamburg 1970), 135.
3   Ministry of Education of the USSR. *On the Main Trends in the
     Field of Education in the USSR in 1968–1970*, 21.
4   Remennikov, B. M. *Ekonomicheskie Problemy Vysshego Obrazo-
     vaniya v SSSR* (Moscow 1968), 77.
5   Ogorodnikov, I. T., 147.
6   Ibid, 151.
7   Nozhko, K., and others, 107.
8   Ibid, 170.
9   Tsentralnoe Statisticheskoe Upravlenie, 539.
10 Ibid, 666, 670.

Bibliography

Bereday, G. Z. F., and others. *The Changing Soviet School* (Boston 1960)
A detailed account of the growth, organisation and working of the Soviet system of education, based upon personal observation and information obtained by a party of American educators during their visit to the USSR in 1960. Contains chapters devoted to all levels of education, the aims, content and methods of school education, educational research, youth organisations and extra-curricular activities.

Bereday, G. Z. F., and Pennar, J. *The Politics of Soviet Education* (London 1960)
A collection of articles on the Party control over schools, class tensions in Soviet education, polytechnic education, problems in the teaching of history, politics and foreign languages in Soviet schools, extra-curricular activities, teacher training, the University of Moscow and selection for, and content of, advanced studies.

Bowen, J. *Soviet Education: Anton Makarenko and the Years of Experiment* (Wisconsin 1962)
A study of Makarenko's life and work against the background of his times, including an assessment of his contribution to educational theory and practice.

Cole, M., and Maltzman, I. *A Handbook of Contemporary Soviet Psychology* (New York 1969)
An advanced book on psychology and research in the fields of developmental psychology, abnormal and social psychology, gen-

eral experimental psychology and higher nervous activity, with important contributions from outstanding Soviet psychologists: Leontiev, Luria, Smirnov, Zaporozhets, Elkonin, Bozhovich, Sokolov and others.

Counts, G. S. *The Challenge of Soviet Education* (New York 1957)
A comprehensive account of Soviet education up to the 1950s, examining the roots and goals of Soviet education, its general, political and moral aspects, the education of the political élite, the transformation of the intellectual class and the training of specialists; considerable effort has been made to interpret educational development against the general political, social and economic background.

Counts, G. S. *Krushchev and the Central Committee Speak on Education* (Pittsburgh 1959)
An analysis of the reform of Soviet education by Khrushchev in 1958, its significance and its substance; includes the full text of the theses of the Twenty-third Congress in English.

Deineko, M. *Public Education in the USSR. Facts and Figures* (Moscow 1956)
A brief exposition of the essential aspects of education in the USSR and the different Soviet republics.

DeWitt, N. *Education and Professional Employment in the USSR* (Washington 1961)
An advanced work prepared for the National Science Foundation, dealing with the Soviet educational system and its relation to the economy of the country, including vocational, semi-professional and professional education and the employment of professional and specialised manpower in the USSR.

DeWitt, N. *Soviet Professional Manpower* (Washington 1955)
An advanced study of the education, training and supply of professional manpower in the USSR in the inter-war period and the post-war period, with numerous tables and charts.

Fitzpatrick, S. *The Commissariat of Enlightenment* (Cambridge 1970)
A detailed study of the early years of education under Lunacharsky and the Narkompros, covering the period from October 1917 till 1921.

Galkin, K. *The Training of Scientists in the Soviet Union* (Moscow 1959)
An account of the institutional set-up in the USSR provided for the training of scientists. Includes the text of the Law on Establishing Closer Links between School and Life and on Further Development of Public Education in the USSR.

Grant, N. *Soviet Education* (London 1964)
A general account of education in the USSR, its organisation, aims, structure, contents and methods. Provides a useful introduction to a variety of aspects of the system, its problems and connections with other aspects of life in the country.

Hans, N. *History of Russian Educational Policy, 1701–1917* (New York 1964)
A detailed description and analysis of progress and changes in the educational policy in Russia from the beginning of the eighteenth century to the October Revolution.

Hans, N. *The Russian Tradition in Education* (London 1963)
An account of the chief contributions to educational thought in Russia from Peter the Great to Khrushchev, where the recent developments are seen as a subtle interaction of Communist ideology and the Russian educational tradition.

Johnson, W. H. *Russia's Educational Heritage* (New York 1950)
A history of Russian education from the fifteenth century to the October Revolution, with the accent upon the growth of various types of educational institution and legal provision and one chapter on the pioneers in Russian educational philosophy.

Kassof, A. *The Soviet Youth Program* (Cambridge, Mass 1965)
A book in the Russian Research Centre Studies Series, containing
a description of the aims, organisation and activities of the Youth
organisations in the USSR, based upon Soviet books, pamphlets
and newspapers. Concluded by the evaluation of activities in
comparison with youth training in other societies.

King, E. J. *Communist Education* (London 1963)
A collection of essays upon a number of educational issues in the
USSR, including the concept of ideology, educational psychology, children at home and at school, teachers' status and role,
polytechnic and higher education.

Korol, A. G. *Soviet Education for Science and Technology* (London
    1957)
A detailed study of the Soviet system of education, the ten-year
schools, secondary specialised schools, the selection, enrolment,
study and graduation in institutions of higher education.

Levin, D. *Leisure and Pleasure of Soviet Children* (London 1966)
A description of the extra-curricular opportunities available to
Soviet children in and out of school, based upon a personal visit
to nine republics, covering artistic, scientific and technical fields,
as well as the Pioneer organisation.

Levin, D. *Soviet Education Today* (London 1963)
An overall account of the school system and important aspects of
education in the USSR.

Meek, D. L. *Soviet Youth, Some Achievements and Problems*
    (London 1957)
A study of a number of aspects of life of the Soviet youth such
as work, leisure, study, marriage and family life, with the help of
numerous extracts from the Soviet press, published in the early
1950s.

Mickiewicz, E. P. *Soviet Political Schools* (New Haven 1967)

A study in political socialisation, based upon original Russian sources, examining the origins and purposes of political education for adults and the institutions involved in it.

Ministry of Education of the USSR. *Public Education in the Soviet Union* (Moscow 1967 and 1968)
A brief description of the recent changes and development of Soviet education, covering in greater detail the last year under consideration.

Ministry of Education of the USSR. *On the Main Trends in the Field of Education in the USSR in 1968–1970* (Moscow 1970)
A description of the trends and tendencies in Soviet education during the two years; produced for the Thirty-second Session of the International Conference on Public Education in Geneva.

Noah, H. J. *Financing Soviet Schools* (New York 1966)
A detailed account of the financing of Soviet education, with an analysis of the sources of funds, budget allocations, preparation of estimates, teachers' salaries and earnings and the wages policy.

Nozhko, K., and others. *Educational Planning in the USSR* (Paris 1968)
An important source of information on educational planning in the Soviet Union, prepared by Soviet experts for UNESCO. Includes also comments by non-Soviet educationists on the Soviet system, on the basis of their visit to the USSR.

Prokofiev, M. A., and others. *Higher Education in the USSR* (Paris 1960)
Three lectures delivered at the International Student Seminar on Higher Education in the USSR, held in Moscow in 1959. The authors examine the growth of Soviet education, its achievements and salient features, as well as the organisation, content and peculiarities of higher technical and humanistic studies in the USSR.

Prokofiev, M. A. *Narodnoe Obrazovanie v SSSR* (Moscow 1967)

A substantial book, describing the progress of education in the USSR since the October Revolution. Includes sections on all levels of education and teachers, and separate chapters on educational development in all the republics of the Union.

Redl, H. B. *Soviet Educators on Soviet Education* (New York 1964)
A collection of articles on the philosophy of education, the family, the school and children in the USSR, by outstanding Soviet writers: Krutetsky, Kovaleva, Makarenko, Krupskaya, Afanasenko, Kairov and others.

Rudman, H. C. *The School and the State in the USSR* (New York 1967)
Part One examines the role of state agencies in the administration of the educational process and includes an analysis of political structures, the relationship of the CPSU to the state and the roles of the State Planning Commission and the Council for the National Economy. Part Two contains a description of the role of the Trade Unions and the Academy of Pedagogical Sciences in the administration and control of education.

Shapovalenko, S. G. *Polytechnical Education in the USSR* (Paris 1963)
An important collection of essays written by Soviet experts on the aims, principles, scope and methods of polytechnic education. The writers include: M. N. Skatkin, I. A. Kairov, S. G. Shapovalenko, N. E. Tseitlin, I. V. Kozyr, P. R. Atutov, A. E. Stavrovsky, L. A. Tsvetkov, M. I. Melnikov, A. A. Shibanov and others.

Shore, M. J. *Soviet Education, Its Psychology and Philosophy* (New York 1947)
A detailed exposition of the evolution of Marxist theory of education from 1850 to the 1950s.

Simon, B. and J. *Educational Psychology in the USSR* (London 1963)

An important collection of longer extracts from the works of well-known Soviet psychologists: Menchinskaya, Elkonin, Kalmykova, Kostyuk, Leontiev, Luria, Teplov, Vygotsky and others.

US Office of Education. *Education in the USSR* (Washington 1957)
A book in the series of studies on foreign systems of education, describing the background, planning, administration, organisation, structure and content of education at all levels in the Soviet Union.

US Office of Education. *Higher Education in the USSR. Curriculum, Schools and Statistics* (Washington 1963)
A review of the reform of education of 1958, followed by a detailed analysis of the curricula in higher education in the USSR, based upon the official curricula published in 1959.

US Office of Education. *Part-time Education in the USSR. Evening and Correspondence Study* (Washington 1965)
Description of the development and the present position of part-time, general, secondary specialised and higher education as well as the informal part-time education for youths and adults, supported by numerous charts and statistical tables, referring to the 1950s and early 1960s.

US Office of Education. *Soviet Commitment to Education* (Washington 1959)
Report of the First Official US Education Mission to the USSR, examining briefly all aspects of education, with a short analysis of the 1958 reform.

US Office of Education. *Soviet Education Programs* (Washington 1960)
A detailed study of the contents of science and mathematics in the schools of general education, polytechnic education, the organisation and operation of school workshops and production training as well as the teacher education in pedagogical institutes and the universities.

Index